ACTIVATE YOUR PSYCHIC ABILITY

ACTIVATE YOUR PSYCHIC ABILITY

THE POWER OF INTUITION REVEALED

PAUL FENTON-SMITH

BLUE ANGEL®
PUBLISHING

ACTIVATE YOUR PSYCHIC ABILITY
The Power of Intuition Revealed

Published by Blue Angel Publishing®
80 Glen Tower Drive, Glen Waverley
Victoria, Australia 3150
Email: info@blueangelonline.com
Website: www.blueangelonline.com

Edited by Cathy Jonas and Jules Sutherland

ISBN: 978-1-922573-91-9

Dedicated to Alexander.

With thanks to my editor Cathy Jonas
for her skills and patience
and to Melinda for her support.

CONTENTS

The names of people used in examples have been changed, along with other details to protect their identities. In some examples, the people described are composites of several people who have similar experiences.

1.
OPENING YOUR EYES TO OPPORTUNITIES

On the honour roll of squandered opportunities, I'm a legend. I've ignored favourable moments and timely openings and cast aside perfectly good ideas to pursue clearly signposted dead ends. Sadly, I'm not the only contender for the list.

Sometimes people don't recognise the unexpected opportunities discovered during meditation or described during clairvoyant readings.

At age 30, Grace was still living with her parents, dreaming of travelling while splurging her income on clothes, personal development courses and a hectic lifestyle. She had twice abandoned saving for a home deposit when she wanted a new car and when expenses became too demanding.

Thriving in her current existence, she felt free and was adamant about not wanting to settle down. Looking ahead to her late 30s, I intuitively saw her with a small boy, aged around three. His wild, dark curls bobbed around as he laughed. He was a soft, kind, sensitive child. Grace is an animal communicator and I noticed that this young boy, probably her son, was practising calling his dog from across the room, using only his thoughts.

While watching television, he would mentally call the dog who was sleeping nearby on a rug. The dark, woolly pup sat up, staring at him. He laughed aloud and threw his head back as the dog bounded over to his side. When I described this scene to Grace, she seemed stressed.

"I'm not sure I want kids," she announced nervously, frowning at the possibility, "I've just got my life the way I like it." Looking further ahead, I saw that she was working from a small home office in the garden, where clients visited with their animals for intuitive readings. Sometimes her boy sat on a dining chair against her office wall, his legs dangling in the air, silently observing while she attuned herself to each pet, describing its home environment and its current health. He sat still and wide-eyed, fascinated by the range of animals that arrived, from dogs and cats to lizards, turtles, mice and wallabies. However, some of the native birds had deafening screeches that made him cover his ears and hastily retreat from the room.

I explained that her son had found a quicker way to retrieve intuitive information about these visitors. He mentally asked his own dog to tell him what was wrong with the client's pet and he received a clear reply almost immediately. As his puppy followed him everywhere while he played alone in the garden, her son was constantly honing his intuitive skills.

"This boy is a natural with animal communication," I told Grace. She seemed worried about the responsibilities ahead of her. While she had trained for years, gradually refining her skills in attuning herself to animals, the child arrived resembling the next generation of software — able to do much more with less time and effort.

"You look relaxed and happy there with your son, your work and in your home," I reminded her, as I sensed that she would have a few sleepless nights coming to terms with what she feared might be a monotonous, suburban life. It was obvious that she loved her vocation and was focused on ways to fine-tune her work with clients and their pets on behavioural issues.

"It all sounds a bit … ordinary," she muttered distastefully.

"Yes, very ordinary. Every child has a mum who reads animals and has vets phoning her after several clients have arrived with clear, accurate details of their pets' health conditions, that are confirmed after scans or blood tests. One veterinarian eventually knows that your referrals make his job easier and he even sends a few pet owners to consult you when he's stumped by particular symptoms. It's such an everyday occurrence that I don't know why I even mentioned it."

I saw her son in the waiting room at the local animal surgery when he was around age five. Tears filled his eyes and trickled down his cheeks as he quietly clutched a large dog that he had never met before.

"What's wrong?" Grace enquired softly.

"I know you always told me not to talk about this outside the house but this dog is going to die today," he whispered. "He wants me to tell his owner goodbye. What do I do?"

Grace hugged her son briefly and then asked the dog's owner if it was okay for him to talk to her about her pet. Shortly afterwards, they were both in tears as the child explained that this big dog was going to join little brown Joey. The owner's dachshund, Joey, had died the previous year after a brief illness. They wept together until the dog struggled up and put his head onto his ageing owner's knee, as if to console her. She held him tightly, sobbing while pressing her face into his fur and told him that she loved him before whispering goodbye.

In the months following her reading, Grace gradually accepted that she might end up with the best of both worlds. The joys of a large garden and friendly neighbours in a suburban life, combined with the rewards of a meaningful career working with animals. She would even have a reliable colleague available for a second opinion when required, at least after school and on weekends.

Many people yearn to experience huge, transformative opportunities like a life-changing lottery win, a dream job arriving without prolonged effort or an unexpected inheritance but it's best to be prepared for smaller openings. These are more frequent and provide practice for noticing potential paths forward in life. It's essential to train with smaller breaks first because sometimes incidental opportunities bring lasting improvements. Several minor refinements each year to ongoing challenges can steadily enhance life.

Frequently, people consult clairvoyants to be shown opportunities that they cannot see for themselves. By learning to gaze beyond daily obstacles, disappointments or frustrating experiences, it's possible to notice hidden possibilities directly. Sometimes this can be done soon after a loss or a challenging ordeal. Often, however, time needs to pass before a person is calm enough to review a difficult experience and examine it objectively for potential possibilities.

Even when intuitively looking ahead at your own life, unexpected events can be easily dismissed as imagination. It's a rare individual who can be completely objective when searching the future for images that reveal outcomes of current personal situations. When teaching intuitive development, the real test of accuracy is when a student reads for a complete stranger and that person confirms the information revealed.

The process of noticing opportunities is no different from becoming aware of intuitive sensations. Both require focus in the moment and awareness of threats and possibilities. Students often experience a high after intuitively scanning for information and relaying information that is confirmed.

Everyone can improve personal intuition with practice, commitment and persistence. It's like learning an instrument. Some people eventually become professional musicians, while others are content to play for pleasure. This book is for people who have had some intuitive experiences and want to know how to strengthen these valuable personal skills so they are fully prepared for when opportunities arrive. The strengths, skills and techniques developed with smaller options can be confidently applied to those rare enormous openings in life, catapulting you towards your goals.

2. INTUITION — A GATEWAY TO BETTER CHOICES

Many of us have made some terrible choices in our lives. From pursuing unsuitable partners to erratic job selections, some individuals seem incapable of discerning what will benefit them and what is simply a path to a dead end. It took a long time for me to realise the value of combining intuition with logic when making decisions, to improve my prospects. In my younger years, every poor choice led me further from my intended path in life, away from the support that accompanies the spiritual light and into the constant struggle of a life lived in darkness.

It's difficult to make good decisions in the dark. Without light for contrast, there are no black-and-white options nor any nuanced shades of grey amidst the alternatives. Everything is hidden and possibilities are invisible. In darkness, only the closest options are discernible and the problem is that the nearest alternatives are not always the best. To glimpse more possibilities, it's necessary to increase the light. Better vision also helps highlight the likely consequences of personal choices.

At 17, I discovered an ancient map of the hand through studying palmistry. A person's hands provide a clear picture of their character traits, talents, life perceptions and suitable career choices. This was one of the first truly useful systems I had seen for navigating my way in life. It was as though someone had turned on a light above me and I could clearly see for the first time.

Over the next decade, I pursued other studies, including meditation, the tarot and astrology, gradually discovering systems for looking ahead to future opportunities. It took another decade to realise the benefits of deep meditation to increase clarity and awareness of more profound options in life.

This process involved awakening my animal intuition. This instinctive perception gradually improved my ability to make better choices and to know which paths might provide long-term fulfilment. Finally, I began developing spiritual intuition. This clarified some of the causes behind current choices and circumstances. It also illuminated the likely long-term consequences of personal decisions. Suddenly I was aware of life's bigger picture, making me more cautious when choosing options.

It's initially dispiriting to have what seems like a brilliant idea for a book or a course only to discover that pursuing it will distract you from your deeper life purpose. It seems contrary to the concept of free will. However, free will is often shaped by past choices, with each decision opening up new possibilities while closing others.

In deep meditative states, it's possible to look ahead further than an initial goal, to see the longer-term after-effects. That great book idea can swallow up two years of your life while steering you away from a possible love relationship, business partnership or a different, more rewarding project. Those other possibilities aren't usually visible when you sketch out the book concept.

When I inwardly requested opportunities or pursued particular goals, I began to ask internally if each option was wise for me spiritually. There's no point in achieving a goal if it is contrary to your deeper purpose in life. That's simply a recipe for misery. Sometimes I ignored the information I received if it said my choice was unsuitable. However, this usually led to undesirable consequences.

This book demonstrates effective techniques for awakening spiritual intuition that can lead to a more spiritually rewarding existence or a life of inner peace and purpose. Awareness of life's bigger picture can reduce stress while increasing personal fulfilment. Developing spiritual intuition doesn't need to change much on the surface of your life. It does, however, mean that more attention is given to emotionally and spiritually nourishing habits that make everyday life more meaningful by replenishing your inner reserves. These practices might include meditation, yoga, swimming, gardening, playing a musical instrument, walking in nature or reading uplifting books.

If life is like growing and maintaining a garden, expanding your personal spiritual intuition is like discovering new, exotic seeds to sprinkle around that garden, with surprisingly good results. Rich colours and fragrances abound, while taller trees provide shade from the hot sun. There are wonderful new tastes, flavours and sustaining foods with surplus fruits, vegetables, herbs and flowers to share.

By combining logic with intuition, it's possible to choose wisely from powerful insight. Making your way through life can be difficult at times, so it's worth embracing every additional tool to improve your personal choices.

Fundamentally, there are four approaches to intuitive reading and each is covered in Chapter 11. By identifying your personal psychic strengths, it's possible to improve these naturally developed areas.

When you become more intuitive, you may find yourself overwhelmed by feelings or senses related to other people or your surroundings. Some effective strategies for psychic sensitivity are covered in Chapter 9. These tools are essential for naturally intuitive people to maintain inner peace and sanity. They can also be taught to others to help an emotionally aware partner or child, so that they don't become uncentred by hyper-awareness of their surrounding circumstances.

Most importantly, by regularly using personal intuition, it's possible to avoid leaving your destiny to chance. Instead of being fatalistic, you can become proactive when exploring your personal options, even choices concealed from view.

3.
DUAL PURPOSES FOR PSYCHIC DEVELOPMENT

By improving your decision-making intuition, it's possible to increase your ability to better predict the outcome of plans or events. This can help with avoiding dead-end jobs or expensive courses that lead nowhere.

When Amy and Dane were searching for a new home, they needed to find a suitable environment in which to raise a family. They didn't want to have to move again until downsizing in retirement. This meant that the property had to suit their immediate needs, including a good school zone, transport links and access to parks and recreation areas. One home they had loved and lost at auction seemed perfect at the time. They felt deflated until six months later when they discovered that three properties that neighboured the house they'd missed out on were about to be demolished for high-rise apartments. They then felt they had been extremely lucky not to have bought that particular house and were inspired to refine their search systems.

After viewing almost 45 homes, they were exhausted and disheartened until Amy devised a plan to simplify the process. She suggested that they both meditate and intuitively look ahead one year to glimpse the house they'd be living in. After the process, they wrote down everything they had seen before sharing it with each other.

After several failed attempts, they both experienced deep

meditations and afterwards compared notes. Dane's list focused on the size of the garage and storage, while Amy's explored the kitchen, the amount of natural light in the house and the location of the children's rooms and walk-in wardrobes. Their written records included an identical bathroom and front door, making it more likely that they would recognise their future home.

Several weeks after this process, Amy and Dane found the house they had seen in their meditations. After some determined negotiating, they purchased it. As they moved in, Amy was puzzled about why she had glimpsed a beautiful new bathroom while their new home contained a shabby 35-year-old one. Dane's response was simple.

"We looked 12 months ahead when you saw it. This means that we have nine months to renovate this ancient relic." Several months later, Amy managed a bathroom renovation that brought the house up to the standard of their intuitive glimpses.

Another reason for psychic development is to nourish the soul or psyche for its journey through life and beyond. By sustaining your soul, you increase happiness and ongoing fulfilment because this alleviates your personal sense of aloneness and quells deep-seated inner hunger for a more meaningful life.

What nurtures your spirit is unique to you. Historically, humans have always sought inner peace and contentment, personal fulfilment, as well as freedom from fear or misery. To achieve this, we have devised different practices, customs, games and processes for spiritual nourishment, ranging from simple regular habits such as daily walks, gardening or creative pastimes to more complex rituals, including meditation, yoga, prayer and self-reflection.

In modern life, people tend to abandon the more difficult processes in favour of simple, effective habits. Few people have time each month for extensive yoga retreats or prolonged fasting and meditating. Grabbing toast for breakfast before racing for the train is the best some can manage on a weekday morning. Many people are time-poor, so short, uncomplicated processes are required.

One powerful advantage of glimpsing the future is to help identify how you can make yourself available for opportunities. There are scant benefits in knowing where events will lead if you're not ready for them when they arrive. Even obstacles intuitively glimpsed can be beneficial, as they give you the opportunity to prepare and prevent the complications of delayed or derailed plans.

Lena, a short, dynamic woman, had recently directed and released a film. Lena wanted to know if it was wise to attend the annual Berlinale Film Festival in Germany in the coming months or if she should fly to Los Angeles to enlist support for her next project. Both were important locations and each presented potential opportunities but Lena only had time and funds for one trip. She was passionate about her work and impatient to advance her career but needed to know which path was best for her professionally.

During this reading, it became apparent that visiting Berlin was a far better option on this occasion, offering a more positive outcome for Lena. Braving the bitter cold of Germany in February, Lena flew to Berlin to attend the festival, where her film won an award. She felt elated and revelled in the interest and attention of hundreds of her peers throughout the festival. During the week following the awards ceremony, she made some valuable contacts in Europe.

"When I attended the opening at the Berlinale Palast, I never expected to appear on stage to accept an award before the festival concluded," she said in a phone call after she returned. "I was walking on air for days. It was brilliant. For a moment, it seemed like every opportunity was available to me."

Because Lena carefully considered her choices, she was present at the festival to accept the prize and prepared to make the most of her visit. She was also able to capitalise on this award through networking opportunities soon after the ceremony. It wasn't necessary to visit Los Angeles for funding as it was offered in Europe. Her newfound contacts invested generously in her next film project, introducing her to brilliant sound engineers, editors and industry professionals. It was as though an enormous door had opened for her, seemingly without effort.

4.
IDENTIFYING LIKELY OUTCOMES

Recently, Steve consulted me because he was considering changing jobs. He worked in IT and had been overlooked twice for promotion, so he decided to look for a new position in a different company. A quick scan of the vacancy ads online made him realise that his current occupation title was rapidly disappearing and that he needed to re-skill to keep up with the pace of change in his industry.

In his first reading, Steve was disappointed to discover that he was unlikely to find a suitable job in his current role at a new company within two years. Instead of leaving the session disappointed, he smiled and said, "To be continued," as he shook my hand and departed.

To his credit, he researched similar positions and discovered his existing job had morphed into a new role that included more coaching and team management. The concept of coaching team members appealed to him, so Steve enrolled in a course and gained a certificate.

In his second work-related reading ten months later, I told Steve that he would eventually work for a well-established, larger organisation but not before he had a brief stint managing a small team of five people. In this short-term role, Steve would have a chance to hone his team management and coaching skills, both of which he would need when working in the larger company.

By the time Steve came for a third reading several months later, he had just begun a lengthy interview process with a large company. He wanted to know if they'd offer him a position. I told him that they were likely to offer him a job, possibly after some delays. The interview process dragged on for almost four months, partly due to temporary funding setbacks in a new project.

A few months after his third reading, Steve phoned again, wanting more clarity about the job-seeking process. Steve was making the most of a difficult progression and being in his early 50s, he was acutely aware that he needed to be on his best game to be hired over the highly skilled younger people also applying for these positions.

During his previous reading, Steve had asked about two new possible companies that had advertised available positions, as both jobs appealed to him. He enquired about the larger company and I told him that they were likely to come back to him with an offer between September and December of that year. In March—three months after that cut-off—although the larger company might still have offered Steve his dream job, he didn't want to wait. As a result, his focus returned to the two positions immediately available.

In this, his fourth reading, I suggested that both companies were likely to offer him a job but that one position would make him happier for the period of time he would be there. I still felt that when his dream occupation was finally offered to him, Steve would resign and take it.

During the process of several separate tarot readings, Steve gradually clarified his career situation and a range of alternatives, plus a possible final outcome. I wondered why this wasn't immediately apparent in his initial reading.

There might be several reasons for this. First, the outcome depended on a range of decisions Steve needed to make prior to the move. Second, he probably became available for new opportunities by being proactive in undertaking additional study and short courses to update his skills and make himself more appealing in the rapidly changing job market. Third, he spent almost 18 months regularly attending conferences and industry events. He explained that he had participated in talks, meetups and other career-related events seven or eight times a month for over a year. This networking helped him to gauge the direction of the industry, learn the latest terminology and introduce him to new ideas, techniques, books and people.

Glimpsing the shifting sands of future opportunities, I decided that during future readings, it was necessary to mentally ask myself this question: "How many chances does this person have at this time to dramatically change the future?" If an individual doesn't like the predicted outcome, there are three questions worth asking themselves:

- Will I enjoy that outcome when it arrives?
- What can I do to avoid that possible result?
- What do I most need to know right now?

Not many clients are as determined to use free will to identify and seize opportunities to the degree that Steve did. Fewer still are prepared to assess the direction of an industry, train up and immerse themselves in the latest approaches over an 18-month period to secure a position that won't be superseded within the next few years. With the pace of change accelerating in many industries, more people will have to proactively retrain or risk redundancy or a downward career trajectory earlier in life than anticipated. Steve mentioned that he expects to have to retrain at least once more before his 60th birthday.

Steve's can-do attitude, hard work and steady determination are important foundations in his current and future job prospects. During his readings, Steve readily accepted his part in making a desired future happen. He saw each reading as a way to ensure he was staying on track towards his goals. When he accepted his next position, he was ecstatic to find, for the first time in his life, he was working with people who respected and supported each other. At least once a week, someone in the workplace acknowledged his efforts and praised or thanked him for something he had done. This encouraged him to respond in kind, noticing and praising the efforts of others and offering support when people needed it.

Sometimes, a consequence that seems far removed from our current desires can turn out to be exactly what is required when circumstances change. However, when a person is anxious about the future and likely to worry or become fixated about a predicted outcome, it's probably best to limit future forecasts to short-term events.

Sometimes, being shown the steps to a goal can ease the concerns about how an objective might be realised.

In a recent reading, Jenny enquired about her daughter. She was worried that her 34-year-old daughter Cate was frustrated with her marriage. Scanning ahead until Cate's early 50s, I saw a table set for a lavish afternoon tea. Eight women sat around it, sipping champagne, chatting exuberantly. It was a simple pre-wedding get-together for someone at the table. Cate opened a card that read, "The first two husbands are just for practice." She laughed heartily at the sentiment and hugged her friend before passing the card around the table.

Cate was about to be married for the third time. It's likely that someone in her 30s doesn't want to hear this before her first marriage. Instead, it's possible to explain to a client that she'll be happily married in her 50s, without mentioning the succession of husbands.

If someone doesn't want a particular consequence, the reader can ask within to be shown what specific decisions or actions might lead directly to that outcome unless deliberately avoided. If the individual is prepared to take responsibility for their personal life direction, it's possible to alter the outcome. To do this, it's necessary to pay attention to actions that encourage undesirable consequences. However, it's important to remember that sometimes a client might actually be very happy with an unwanted outcome long after a prediction. People grow and as they do, personal needs change. Someone who was your dream partner when backpacking through Europe when you were young and free might not be the ideal companion to grow old with.

MEASURING THE ACCURACY OF INTUITIVE IMAGES

When Ingrid asked about her next home, I described a three-bedroom house with a large, established garden at the back. The garage had been converted to a home office, with two enormous skylights and French doors opening to a small deck containing a table and a single chair overlooking the lawn. Ingrid seemed puzzled as she shook her head.

"No. That can't be right. We're currently looking at two-bedroom apartments by the beach. We want cafés and clubs close by and public transport at the front door." What Ingrid didn't realise was that in a month, she would discover that she was expecting their first child. Raising a family in a neighbourhood with constant traffic and noisy nightlife probably wouldn't be their first choice.

When she returned four years later, Ingrid explained that her second child was due in three months. She wanted to know if it was best to extend her current home or relocate to a bigger property. Her husband didn't want to move, as he had recently renovated his garage home office, adding a small kitchen and bathroom.

There are two simple methods for measuring the likelihood of a glimpsed image being accurate. With the first, if a scene seems surprising or unlikely, I mentally return my focus to the client and the room for 10 seconds. (This occurs naturally if you're gazing out an open window into the distance and suddenly a bee flies in the room, for example. In a moment, your awareness shifts from distant scenery to avoiding the immediate threat of a bee sting.)

If, after focusing on the room briefly, the same image is still in my mind's eye when I resume intuitively scanning ahead, I know that it's not my imagination and I tell the person what I can internally see.

The second process involves seeing a gauge in my mind's eye that displays—from zero to 100—how likely the current prediction is to occur. This requires persistent practice to avoid imagining a preferred result. As I observe the gauge, I ask about the accuracy of the scene I have glimpsed. It can then swiftly move down towards 'unlikely' or up towards 'very likely' and I know how much I can tell the client.

SIMPLE AWARENESS EXERCISE

To demonstrate this process of shifting awareness in intuitive development classes, I ask for a volunteer and we sit on two chairs, a metre apart, facing each other. I stretch out one arm, forming a fist with the first finger pointed towards the ceiling. I ask the volunteer to focus on themself. Then I instruct them to gradually shift their focus to my extended finger. When this happens, the student is less aware of themself and more focused on my finger.

Next, I ask them to extend their focus or awareness away from my finger to me. Now they are unaware of themself and of my finger. Instead, they are increasingly aware of only me. Then I ask them to narrow their focus back to my finger, excluding awareness of me. For the purpose of this exercise, the student's awareness is brought back to my hand and outstretched finger. After a few minutes, I ask them to draw their awareness back to themself so that they are no longer aware of me, my hand or my finger.

In tarot readings or psychic sessions, a reader usually begins each session focused on themself. Gradually, they'll move personal awareness away from themself to their tools. These might be cards on a table, an object they're holding (such as a ring or watch) or simply a list of the client's questions.

Next, the reader moves their awareness to the client, focusing on that individual for the rest of the reading. Sometimes, such as in a card reading, the reader will bring their awareness back to the cards, shuffling and repositioning them for a new question before refocusing on the client.

At the end of the session, the reader retracts personal awareness into their own body as the client departs. This simple exercise shows what occurs in a psychic reading. Any time you feel at a loss, or you're grappling with a block, simply retract your awareness within and then slowly refocus on the client.

If it's a distance reading and you don't have a client on screen, you can request a headshot for reference. If you don't have an image as an anchor, you'll probably have a question list from the client to work with.

If so, focus on one question at a time.

Once you're aware of another person, it's possible to extend your awareness to the surrounding room or even the whole building. Eventually, it's possible to extend your awareness to that person's current life circumstances. After this, it's not difficult to extend your awareness into another person's life and move it back to past events and forward to future situations.

The steps for awareness focus are as follows:

1. Awareness of self.
2. Become conscious of another person.
3. Become aware of another person's current life circumstances.
4. Increase focus on past events from another person's life.
5. Shift focus to future events in another person's life.
6. Return awareness to yourself.

WHEN PREDICTIONS DON'T EVENTUATE

One particular client, Mona, has readings with me periodically. During each session, she will ask about a new potential job, partner or life direction — and then take herself in the opposite direction to any successful outcome I predict.

After a recent reading, I felt frustrated. I wondered why Mona even returned for more readings when things rarely eventuated as predicted. If I consulted a clairvoyant who was clearly incorrect about major questions on several occasions, I'd find a different psychic. Was she waiting for me to predict a miracle? Did she have a powerful subconscious resistance to positive opportunities, or did she simply enjoy telling me that what I had previously predicted didn't eventuate?

Mona reminds me of the use of free will. After her most recent reading, I asked a guide in meditation why so few of my predictions for Mona eventuate. He suggested that Mona resists being told what will become of her, so being told what to expect in the future sometimes triggers unconscious resistance to opportunities. He also mentioned that Mona was very stuck in her life and had been since she was very young. The only area where Mona truly succeeds is in her career, where she is focused, hard-working and competent.

Despite feeling it's unsafe to thrive in front of others, Mona accepts that it's still possible for her to find work and support herself. It's likely that the event that triggered this belief occurred before her working life and consequently did not shape her career attitudes. Our attitudes to home, relationships and self-worth are often shaped in our preschool and school years, whereas career beliefs are usually shaped in adulthood when we have more resources to negotiate better outcomes. Both can be reshaped if required.

Finally, my guide explained that Mona returned for readings because a very small part of her wants to be inspired and to be told that there are positive opportunities ahead for her. Having an optimistic reading is like being able to take one long deep breath after being underwater for an extended period. I began to consider if it was time to tell Mona what was more likely to occur despite my predictions but my guide advised against this.

"Don't tell her that she'll be stuck for another two years. Deep down, she already knows this. She has tried many times to find a way out of her restrictions but has been unsuccessful so far. Your readings for Mona are not about being accurate. It's just your ego that wants you to be correct. In each reading, you become a person who lights a candle of hope for her. You notice that she's stuck and you offer her compassion and optimism. It soon fades away but the memory of the kindness sustains her for days or weeks afterwards. She would love to have a weekly session with you but she is also afraid that too many readings might make them lose their potency to give her brief periods of hope when she needs them most.

"If you want to help her more, find a small step she can take towards freedom. It might seem like an incremental measure to you but everyone makes limited progress before being able to proceed rapidly towards personal goals. We all crawl in order to walk before we can run."

I felt humbled to hear this and determined to offer Mona all the kindness I could when she visited next. My guide also reminded me that sometimes in the reading process, it's possible to awaken spiritual awareness in clients or reignite a desire to pursue personal knowledge or nourishment beyond the reading process. "It's not always about predicting the future," he gently reminded me.

WHEN READINGS ARE NOT FOCUSED ON PREDICTIONS

Sometimes people consult readers for unexpected reasons. When reading for a woman in her 70s recently, I clairvoyantly glimpsed an intelligent person who gave up a promising career for family life. After her children left home and moved interstate, she felt unfulfilled. It wasn't simply an empty nest that she faced but a cavernous spiritual void. As I described it to her, she produced a small, checked handkerchief and wiped her eyes.

Collette explained that she had spent the previous decade exploring spiritual alternatives with a wide range of groups but always felt like an outsider. She then mentioned that during an overseas holiday, while out walking one afternoon, she sat on a rocky outcrop and stared at the ocean for an hour. The tranquil water ebbed and flowed, with only the occasional wave breaking the surface. Without warning, a vision of a man appeared before her. She sat, frozen, as she scrutinised his outline while looking through him at the ocean.

"Who are you?" she mentally asked.

"Don't you know? Have you forgotten me?" he asked in return. After a minute or two, he was gone again. I asked her who she thought he might have been but she was confused.

"I think it was Jesus but I'm not religious and never go to church."

"It's possible that this person is your living or deceased spiritual mentor. Maybe you're not an outsider after all? Perhaps you're already on someone's list and there is a guide waiting to assist you with your spiritual journey."

When Collette was leaving, I gave her a copy of a book to read, explaining that it might help her to make sense of what she had seen that day. She emailed the following day to say that she was already halfway through the book, and yes, it had clarified several questions she had been asking.

Her email prompted me to ask what she had come for, aside from predictions. Upon reflection, it seems that Collette came to have someone acknowledge that she had made a selfless choice as a young woman but that now it was time to consider her own development. During a clairvoyant session, it doesn't really matter if a person needs a reading, a book, recognition for past sacrifices or unbiased attention if a reader fulfils that need on the day.

In classes, students are reminded that readers can't truly know if they've helped clients or exactly how they have inspired or supported them. I had forgotten that sometimes a reading is not always about predictions. Occasionally, it's simply an opportunity for two people to sit together to focus on a satisfactory path to peace and fulfilment. Sometimes, it's a chance to help another person refocus on the spiritual development underlying life's everyday demands. Occasionally, it's good to have a stranger help you to make sense of your life, even if they only put one or two pieces of the jigsaw into place.

5. INTUITIVE IMAGES — WHAT DO YOU SEE?

Some students struggle with intuitive images—clairvoyance—because they expect to see pictures with their eyes. Clairvoyant scenes or snapshots appear in the mind's eye — the same place you perceive remembered scenes. When recalling a favourite beach, a romantic holiday or a dog you had as a child, it's likely that you'll have those pictures in your mind's eye. Clairvoyant images are very much like remembered or imagined mental impressions, which is why it's necessary to be vigilant not to stray from intuitive visions to pure imagination.

Sometimes when the connection between psychic and client is poor, the reader doesn't mentally see an image of the person who is significant to the client. Instead, they'll see someone they know who resembles that person. If a brief description of the person in their mind's eye is outlined, the client might recognise the friend or co-worker. If a more precise description is given, it is less likely to resemble the client's friend. When the connection is strong, it's easier to be more exact with observations because the details intuitively received are sharper in the mind's eye.

With a strong psychic connection to the client, it's also easier for the practitioner to intuitively move forward or back in time or consciously zoom in for more details. In one tarot reading, a woman asked about love relationships. The cards on the table included the King of Wands, so I described a bold, assertive man who was naturally competitive, forthright, cheeky and someone who thrived on a challenge.

"That describes all three of the men I'm dating," she said, unblinking. Scanning through the seven cards on the table, I noticed The Emperor card and suggested that he might be an Aries.

"That's down to two, now," she responded. I tuned in clairvoyantly to clarify her situation and moved forward 12 months to see who was around her then. I described a man who had his own business and she confirmed that both of these Aries men owned businesses. I told her that he had two teenage children and it turned out that both men had two children. Realising that this process might take half of our reading time, I scanned the man's body for physical scars, moles or other identifying marks. I told her that he had a thin scar from a childhood accident on his right shin, near his ankle. It was around 5 cm long. She said she would study them both in the coming days to see who was most likely to become her long-term partner.

"You realise that if neither man has a scar, you might meet another Aries with two teenage children and be with him in 12 months," I added. She laughed, delighted at the possibility.

The clearer the link to a person, the more accurate the images appear. A client recently returned for a reading and explained that several years previously, I had described a potential partner to her. She said that I described him as tall, quick-minded and successful in his career. She mentioned that I had glimpsed him standing in an orchard of apples and pears. I had explained to her in the previous reading that this was not a home orchard but a large, commercial enterprise.

Before her recent reading, she said that she had met this man but that the orchard he owned was an almond orchard. Yes, the property covered several hundred acres and although she had not been to visit the orchard, she wasn't aware of any apple or pear trees.

I explained to her before the recent reading that when I see images, they are usually literal. They are as you might see them in person. I'm not someone who received cryptic or symbolic images. After her reading, I began to think about why I might have described an apple and pear orchard instead of an almond one, especially considering their distinctly different leaf shapes.

First, her new partner might have a small fruit orchard close to the homestead, with the almond orchard beginning further away from the house. Almond trees generally require less attention than apple and pear trees as the fruit ripens. Second, if the intuitive connection I have to the client is not strong, I sometimes see an image in my mind's eye that is not accurate but the closest memory I have of what a person or a situation looks like. Third, he may not have been standing in his own orchard when I glimpsed him in the earlier reading. Although this wasn't the reason, sometimes it's difficult to determine leafless trees intuitively glimpsed in winter when they are deciduous.

The reader doesn't always have the luxury of time to explore an image during the reading process. If the client cannot make sense of the image I'm describing, I move on. Afterwards, they sometimes ask me to clarify something I've said months or years previously but I usually cannot even recall the reading at that point. It's sometimes difficult to explore or expand on an image two minutes after you've glimpsed it as that thread of information has slipped from view. It's sometimes like being on a train, travelling at speed through the countryside. The views out the window are constantly changing.

If these intuitive images are vague or scattered, it's important to take a few moments to become centred and improve the connection. Sometimes when reading, I feel centred, but the client is scattered. They may have been frustrated by heavy traffic, had a bad day at work or be exhausted from struggling with ongoing personal issues. In these instances, a kind word, a glass of water or giving the client all of my attention is sometimes sufficient to help them settle for the reading.

IMPROVING CLAIRVOYANCE SKILLS

A powerful way to improve clairvoyance skills is to focus closely on what you are seeing. Most people are busy and don't have time to sit still long enough to notice a view, a flowering hedge by the side of the road or a cat asleep on the roof of a car. It's not enough to simply see. It's important to be able to absorb as many details as possible when glimpsing fleeting visions. Try this with the image below.

Take five seconds to examine the following photograph. Then cover it up from view.

Image by milla1974

- Did you notice that not all the sunflowers were facing the same direction? I've heard many people say how sunflowers follow the sun all day and always face a direction in unison but this is not entirely accurate.
- Were you aware that not all of the flowers had opened up when this photograph was taken?
- How many flowers were only partially unfolded? Were you conscious of the colour at the centre of each flower? When the flowers are green or yellow in the centre, they are fresh blooms. After bees have been through to pollinate, the young sunflowers gradually turn black in the centre, revealing the sunflower seeds.
- Was the sky clear or overcast?

This is a simple picture without too many unique objects or people. Now try this process with the slightly more complicated image below.

Take 10 seconds to look closely at the photo and then cover it up. Then read the questions overpage.

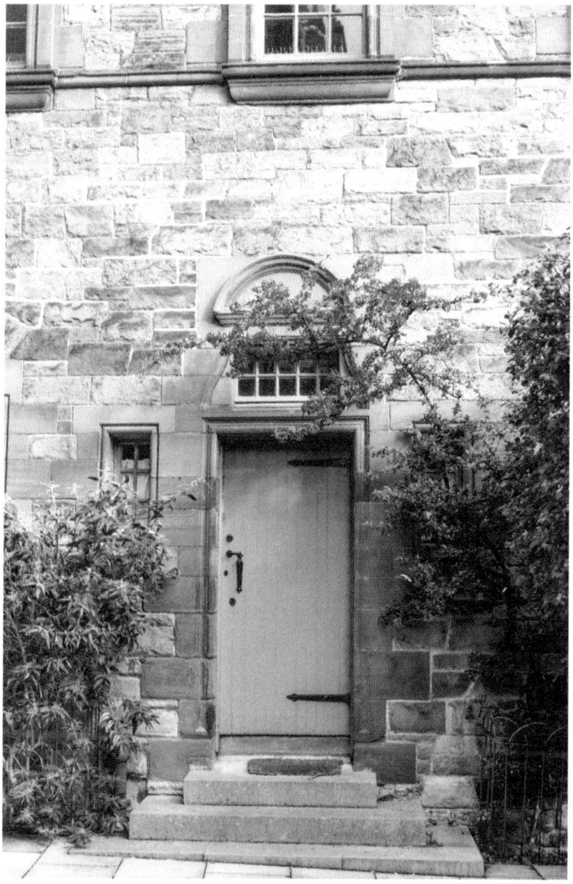

Image by Lucija Ros (Unsplash)

This is an image of the front door of a home. If you were to describe this to a client who has not yet seen this property, you'd need to be as clear as possible so that the person could recognise the location on first viewing. Precision is essential because the house is probably in a long line of similar properties in a town crammed with houses made from the same stone.

- How many windows are visible in this image?
- What are the steps leading to the house made from?
- What colour is the front door?
- What colour is the front door handle?
- Is there a mat at the front door?
- What colour are the flowers overhanging the front door?
- Are there any windows in the front door?
- What colour is the stonework across the front of the property?

Most people cannot answer every question accurately from a 10-second viewing. It took me three viewings to notice the arch over the front door and the tiny spikes at the base of the upstairs windows to deter birds. With practice and a variety of images, it's possible to improve personal visual abilities and memory for glimpsed scenes.

As your optical memory improves, select a photograph or image randomly and glance at it for five to ten seconds. Then take a notepad or tablet and list what you remember from each picture. Then look back at the image to see what you noticed and what was missed. Repeat this process three to five times in succession to gauge if your powers of observation and memory retention improve.

When scanning through images of a person's life in a reading, they flash through the mind's eye rapidly, so attention is required to determine when a scene is important and to pause to focus on what is happening at that point in the person's life. Highlights somehow seem brighter to me when I scan through the years.

In a recent reading for 46-year-old Jorge, I scanned backwards from 45 to 35 but nothing stood out to me.

"This is strange," I said aloud. "I'm scanning back through the months and years and I don't see any highlights. It's as though every day is the same. Did life feel like this to you over the past eight to ten years?"

"Well, yes," he said, deliberately pointing to the recorder. I paused it and he explained he had been in prison for seven years from age 35 and that returning to life afterwards was proving slow and difficult. He was unable to find steady work and the days seemed tedious and repetitive. I immediately realised how important it was to scan ahead for better times, new opportunities and what might give his life purpose.

With practice, it's possible to ask a question and allow your intuition to find the answer by supplying an image in the mind's eye.

When reading for Rosa, I had a strong intuitive connection, so when she asked why she didn't trust her own judgement, I was able to mentally request to be shown an incident or a situation that influenced her trust in herself. I intuitively saw her at home as an 11-year-old. A shy child, she retreated into books and drawing when overwhelmed and home was her sanctuary. Being emotionally sensitive to people's agendas and her surroundings, she often felt overwhelmed in crowds or around new people.

A visitor was at her house. This charming, charismatic man in his early 30s was a friend of her parents and they welcomed him. However, he had an unnatural attraction to their young daughter and was searching for a moment to be alone with her.

Rosa sensed his intentions and couldn't understand why her parents liked him or trusted him enough to allow him into the house. Unable to express her fears to her parents, she began to doubt her own judgement. I confirmed the accuracy of her instincts so that she might be reminded that her judgement was correct.

Sometimes that's what intuition is — being able to notice details that others overlook. The fact that Rosa's parents didn't notice their guest's agenda weakened Rosa's self-confidence, leaving her feeling that she imagined bad intentions about someone she didn't know. My reminder about her accurate judgement might begin the process of trusting and rebuilding her intuitive instincts.

Sometimes, people manage to keep secrets and maintain lies by diverting the attention of others and by weakening others' trust in their personal instincts. When this occurs, remember that others cannot lie to you unless you also agree to lie to yourself. This means ignoring your instincts.

The next time I saw Rosa, she enthusiastically told me how her intuition was flowing freely through dreams and sensing the emotions of people around her. Her reading was the beginning of a lifelong pursuit of intuitive and spiritual knowledge.

6. WHY LEAVE YOUR DESTINY TO CHANCE?

Spiritual intuition provides clarity about the consequences of intended actions. It can also be used to tailor your personal efforts towards specific goals. If the planned path is unlikely to lead to your desired objective, simply ask, "What changes do I need to make to achieve this outcome?" or, "Is this the most suitable goal for me at this time?" Then it's essential to relax, calm the mind and listen carefully within for the answers.

This is where intuition helps people glimpse the consequences of their intended actions before taking all of the steps. Knowing ahead of time that a project, trip or plan won't provide a rewarding outcome can save time, money and effort while helping to avoid disappointment.

Occasionally, I'm inspired to write a book based on an idea that seemed fantastic at the time. When I intuitively explore the likely outcome, if it's not worthwhile, I'm initially disappointed. Then I remember that by not pursuing it, I have effectively saved time, effort and money that I can devote to more meaningful projects. As I'm on the wrong side of 50, every decision I make going forward needs to be precise and beneficial because I don't have decades ahead to explore new directions.

For this examination of future outcomes to be effective, it requires a series of carefully worded questions. Each enquiry helps narrow the focus towards discovering the best path to a desired objective or the most fulfilling goal to pursue. If the answer is no, it's not the end of the process. Instead, maybe the question needs to be refined.

Susan, a fledgling writer, had written a screenplay throughout a long, dreary winter and wanted it made into a film. Here are some sample questions that she posed about her project:

- Is it wise to make a film with Toby next year? (Answer: No.)
- Is it wise to make a film next year? (No.) This question eliminates Toby from the process.
- Is it wise for me to make a film in the next two years? (No.) This extends the timeline.
- Can this screenplay be made into a successful film? (No.) This opens up the possibility of offering the screenplay to a filmmaker to produce.
- Is this project better off being rewritten as a novel? (No.)
- Is writing a part of my career in the future? (Yes.) This broader question is designed to determine if the client is wasting time pursuing writing as an occupation.
- What form will my writing career take in the future?
- Is it beneficial to find a writing teacher or coach this year? (Yes.)
- Is it a valuable use of time to attend a writing course this year? (No.)
- Is it worthwhile to attend a writers' support group in the coming year? (Yes.)

With this line of questioning, Susan discovered that plans to make a film with or without Toby in the coming year were likely to prove fruitless. She's understandably reluctant to waste time and money on a possible dead end. She has also clarified that rewriting the current screenplay as a novel is unlikely to end successfully. Through this process, it is clear that she does have a career ahead as a writer if she engages the services of a writing teacher or coach and joins a writers' support group.

Having gleaned this information about the consequences of her actions, Susan still has the option of pursuing the film-making project with Toby or concentrating on improving her creative skills in other directions. Although writing is primarily a solitary pastime, she realised through the use of spiritual intuition that a support group and a writing coach can help her towards her long-term goal of becoming a paid content creator. Progress might be slow at first but strengthening her skills now could be useful later in life. The earlier Susan refines her skills and technique, the longer career life she has as a screenwriter or novelist.

Susan's creative success depends not only on glimpsing the future she desires but also in regular practical effort to write, hone her skills and improve her techniques. Later, when she has completed a book or a play, she can seriously consider publication of her work.

Glimpsing the outcome of intended actions doesn't eliminate the need for physical effort to make a goal real. Books don't write themselves and a first draft is not a completed project. Experienced writers know that a work is never actually complete. It's not done when it has been edited or even published because it can be changed in later editions, translated into another language or made into a film or documentary.

Taking control of our personal destiny requires routinely pausing to reassess goals because small changes are easier when applied regularly. It's important to assess current methods for achieving those aims and personal objectives. Asking if there's a better way to do this can shorten the effort required to achieve goals because it's possible to find the most direct path up the mountain without time wasted with detours or unnecessary distractions. The frustrating results of devoting months or years to a project that eventually stalls are dispiriting.

Naturally, the effectiveness of this process is dependent on being detached from the desired outcome when asking questions about your own future. If this is impossible, it might be necessary to consult someone more objective to ask questions about your goals and life direction. If finding a suitable person for this task is difficult, it's time to start an intuitive development support group. This is like a writers' group, but instead, participants meditate together, then pair off to answer each other's questions on a regular basis.

With habitual meditation, it becomes easier to focus on a project repeatedly, writing down your observations and answers to personal questions immediately after each meditation. With practice, it's easier to notice when a particular method has stilled your conscious mind sufficiently to access precise, accurate information about future events, outcomes and influences on plans.

Many people find that clear, deep meditations with a strong connection to the higher self occur only sporadically. Regular time set aside for contemplation is still necessary to maintain the skills. With practice, these profound meditations occur more frequently. Recording each session in a diary or an iPad preserves those brilliant, sharp meditations that result in crystal-clear images, scenes and information. Even a single fantastic reflection period a year can provide vast amounts of information and life-changing glimpses of events ahead. It can also inspire more persistent effort with personal development.

To improve the process, try asking these questions when next enjoying a deep, calm connection with your higher self:

Questions to Improve Intuitive Ability

- How can I improve my meditations to strengthen my spiritual connection?
- What is the most effective way to access my intuition? Is it visually, auditorily or through physical body sensations?
- What desires, circumstances, or people decentre me and reduce my intuitive accuracy?
- Would a change in diet, habits, routines, or home environment improve my intuitive abilities?
- How can I increase my intuitive sensitivity without becoming regularly drained by people and circumstances?

All the careful thinking and planning in the world can still leave your destiny to chance if you don't intuitively look ahead to ensure the current path leads to your desired goal.

Some of my most successful clients who own businesses seek my services as a consultant when planning new ventures. Theo owns a number of restaurants and cafés in Europe. After he has found a suitable venue, negotiated a lease and selected a manager for the venture, he phones me to see if his plans will end successfully. I recognise his deep, gravelly voice and the distinctive Middle Eastern accent immediately when he enquires about available times for a session.

Experience has taught Theo that the planned construction of a tall building nearby, an ongoing issue with local planning authorities, an obstructive landlord or even a poor choice of manager can cost him dearly. He has lost millions of euros over the years with all of these issues and doesn't want to repeat past mistakes. Poor staff choices have previously been his most costly oversights.

During distance readings, Theo occasionally asks about two or three staff members by name to ensure that they'll protect his investment when he's not there. He's a man who is proactive and vigilant about his future. His continued success through economic winters proves that his approach works well for him. While maintaining a close focus on his businesses and staff, Theo also keeps abreast of food industry trends to ensure his efforts are not wasted.

7. TOOLS TO IMPROVE INTUITIVE FOCUS

Even experienced clairvoyants have bad days. I trained with Christine, a brilliant medium in the UK, many years ago and one day, when I called in to collect her for a day out, she was distraught. She had lost her keys and couldn't leave the house without them.

"I've meditated, asked them in spirit and nothing!" she sighed. I made myself a cup of Earl Grey tea while she turned over piles of papers and stacks of books and opened every kitchen cabinet in search of her keys. It was a small three-bedroom apartment, so I figured that she would uncover her keys in a few minutes. I didn't realise she had been searching for them for several hours. I knew she needed help if we were to leave the apartment together that day.

"Do you have a tarot deck?" I asked calmly.

"What?"

"A tarot deck. Do you have one in the house?" She walked away, shaking her head, appearing a few minutes later with a pristine deck of cards. As she returned to her bedroom to continue the hunt, I sat on the living room carpet and shuffled the deck. I asked a short list of specific questions to identify the location of the house keys.

- Are Christine's house keys currently inside this apartment? (Yes.)
- Are Christine's house keys currently in the living room? (No.)
- Are Christine's house keys currently in her kitchen? (No.)
- Are Christine's house keys currently in her bedroom? (Yes.)

- Are Christine's house keys contained within something and not easily visible? (Yes.)
- Are Christine's house keys currently in her handbag? (No.)
- Are Christine's house keys currently inside an item of clothing? (Yes.)
- Are Christine's house keys currently inside a coat pocket? (Yes, but be adaptable.)

"Yes, however, be adaptable," suggested that Christine's keys were inside a coat but not necessarily inside a coat pocket. I asked her what coat she had worn the previous day and she pointed to a brown, woollen, knee-length coat on the floor of her room. I picked it up and rifled through the pockets but didn't find the keys. I then held the coat tightly and shook it vigorously. The jingle of her keys was clear. I then felt around the base of the coat and found them. They had slipped through a tear in the coat pocket lining and ended up at the base of her coat.

"How on earth did you find them?" she asked.

"I asked my guides to ask your guides to ask the key fairy," I replied with a grin.

"Cheeky sod …" She playfully slapped me. "I spent half a day looking for them before you arrived. I'm exhausted. I can't go anywhere now."

"What you need is an early lunch and I know just the place," I said, ignoring her decision to stay home. An hour later, we were laughing across a table covered with warm bagels, salad and a pair of teapots. We were both relaxed. Christine was happy because she had forgotten the frustrating morning and I was calm because I had her house keys safely inside my backpack.

Sometimes intuitive tools help narrow down an issue or focus attention where it is required to produce a clear answer. In this instance, Christine's keys were still inside her apartment. Had they been somewhere else, we might not have found them again.

When I arrived at her flat, Christine was beyond being able to sit still in quiet meditation to ask about her keys. She was ready to burn the place down and walk away. Using the tarot enabled me to ask a series of specific questions, narrowing them down until I became focused on one particular item of clothing.

I chose to use the tarot in that situation because it is particularly effective for specific questions. Meditation wouldn't have been as effective for me here because Christine kept walking into the room complaining about life and her missing keys. Had I been a Zen master, it probably would not have mattered but I could not muster that level of focus. It helps to have an assortment of predictive tools and systems for a range of situations.

Clairvoyance was the best choice for Kieran, who asked a general question about his health. In his late 60s, he was carrying some extra weight but appeared to be well until I intuitively scanned down through his body.

The first glimpse revealed an almost 15-cm scar down his chest. When I described it, he said that he didn't have a scar at the front but did have one in the same position at the back. I searched again and saw it at the front, so I guessed that it was yet to come.

I mentioned prostate issues which he confirmed. Then on closer examination, I saw a medical person training a small laser on his prostate before giving him several short bursts of treatment. Kieran explained that this laser was a recent acquisition of a hospital in Sydney and the first of its type in Australia.

Next, I intuitively saw a similar laser being used just above and to the right of the navel. It was a strange image. When turned on, it was as if the laser light only existed for 2 cm inside his body. It wasn't visible between the machine and his skin, nor beyond the area it was treating. Then gradually, the properties of the beam changed. I noticed a thin, straight line of light, widening like an umbrella for about 2 cm inside the area to be treated, which then resumed its original shaft-like appearance afterwards.

I saw him chatting to an attendant during a follow-up session. The person was excited by the results and summoned two colleagues to examine a scan on screen. Then I intuitively saw Kieran say, "I have an issue with my big toe. It's a painful ingrown toenail. Can you use the laser on that?"

The response was, "I don't know. I guess we could try." At this, Kieran laughed, explaining that he actually did have a painful toe and it's the sort of question he might ask if buoyed by the success of recent treatment.

Looking ahead, I noticed a different type of laser being used to trim some calcification around his spine several years later. This was an alternative to surgery and with a shorter convalescence, which seemed to appeal to Kieran.

With practice, you'll know what tools or intuitive approaches suit each different situation. Some psychics begin personal readings by holding a piece of a client's jewellery to form a psychic cord to the person and kick-start the reading process. Others commence each session by glancing at a person's palms as an entry point. When an intuitive connection is established, information usually flows smoothly. A wide range of intuitive tools improves results when using personal intuition to refine decisions or help others find clarity.

Tools are also useful for those days when an urgent decision is required after a poor night's sleep or when a client arrives in a state of mental chaos and cannot focus on one issue at a time. Effective systems improve accuracy when it's most needed, allowing for positive decisions that help life return to normal. In professional practice, tools and systems improve consistency, ensuring that clients receive clear readings despite clairvoyants' occasional bad days.

8. GLIMPSING THE FUTURE WITHOUT TOOLS

Occasionally, when reading for someone, information flows easily, almost effortlessly. In these moments, a clairvoyant can go beyond the tools and systems to mine a deep vein of valuable information. It's suddenly possible to speak freely, describing scenes and situations that bear no resemblance to the person's current life, yet they still feel sharp, tangible and real. Some students fear releasing the familiar tools and structured systems, so in advanced courses, there are a few exercises to encourage them to dive from a sturdy cliff into the cold, deep, clear waters of a river below.

In tarot masterclass courses, there is a demonstration reading where a student volunteer asks a specific question. We discuss the question before any cards are selected to ensure everyone knows what is being asked. As the person selects each card, it is placed image down on the table so that none of the card faces are visible. Students then decide what the answer is to the question without seeing the card images, using only their intuition. Then they write their findings down on paper. These notes are for their eyes only. I then read the cards, one by one, giving my interpretation aloud without turning any of them over. Essentially, this reading is conducted without identifying any of the cards selected.

Afterwards, students are invited to discuss what I've said, what they sensed and if they disagree with the information provided.

Someone usually asks to see the faces of each card to check accuracy but when the cards are turned over, every card is blank. I have a blank deck specifically for this purpose.

"How will we know if we are accurate?" is the immediate reaction.

In real readings, there is rarely any certainty about accuracy. Much of what we talk about when giving predictions hasn't yet happened, so the only way to know with certainty is when clients return for another reading and tell us that we were previously correct. At that point, we often can't recall what we have previously told them. It's useful to forget readings soon after sessions conclude to release the energy of that session and not take it into another reading where it might affect personal perception.

When practitioners cannot forget a session, it's often a sign that they were emotionally triggered by what was seen in the reading or that they have not properly severed a psychic cord to the client after the reading concluded. Remaining unbiased requires a psychic to release previous sessions and to clearly focus on each new client.

9. STRATEGIES FOR SENSITIVITY

Naturally sympathetic people can easily become uncentred by their immediate environments. If, while standing in a crowd, a person is intuitively aware of the emotions of the people around them, there is a risk of getting swept away on a tide of conflicting unspoken hopes, fears and resentments. When this happens, a person tends to feel fuzzy-headed, physically tired, unfocused and uncoordinated. In these states, they can become accident-prone and less spatially aware or conscious of their surroundings. To alleviate this, it is essential to manage personal sensitivity when surrounded by grief, anger or chaos. Unspoken emotions can be more influential than feelings that are openly acknowledged, especially for intuitively impressionable people.

Sensitive individuals regularly feel immersed in the resentment, grief, fear, anger, sadness or loneliness of people in close proximity. They are often unable to distinguish between their own feelings and the emotions of others, due to porous boundaries. It's impossible to stay dry when falling into a swimming pool. Likewise, a sensitive person can feel utterly submerged in the pervasive feelings of others without prior warning.

If a family member is grieving the loss of a friendship or relationship and acknowledges this, it's an authentic process. Other people in the household expect this forlorn person to be less sociable, more easily irritated by frustrations and less interested in participating in group activities. However, when sorrow, anger or frustrations are habitually concealed, it can be emotionally draining for people who are sensitive to these inescapable emotional undercurrents.

In my 20s, I shared rental houses and quickly discovered what worked for me and what didn't. Loud phone conversations overheard from another room could be negated by soft music, flowing water—such as a garden sprinkler or fountain—or an open window that provided distant sounds of traffic. Occasionally, the roar of a crowd from a local sports field sufficed.

In one terraced house I shared with two others, when a co-tenant was grieving, I felt immersed in her emotions. To protect myself, I retreated to the sunroom to write. I played classical music (my housemates soon tired of listening to Berlioz compositions) and lay on my chaise in the dappled sunlight. If it wasn't possible to concentrate or I felt uncentred by my environment, I read Oscar Wilde poetry or cleaned the sunroom from floor to ceiling to ensure my immediate environment was thoroughly purified. We only had a tiny concrete backyard that was shaded by the tall warehouse next door, so it wasn't possible to escape into the sunshine or the serenity of a garden.

Simple strategies for avoiding emotional undercurrents include taking a walk or escaping into the garden or a local park. If sounds are distracting, such as a nearby argument or builders working next door, noise-cancelling headphones might help. Sensitive people are especially affected by sounds, foods, unexpressed grief or people with profound internal hunger. Spiritual emptiness can be a combination of hollowness, aloneness and dread. It's not that a person can't reach out to others for support but that the individual doesn't even seem to know that other people might provide support. The person feels isolated and stuck, experiencing a profound emptiness that nothing seems to satisfy.

Julius felt keenly aware of the emotional emptiness within himself and his siblings throughout his childhood. As an adult, he is careful to avoid living with people who are spiritually starving. He finds that being aware of another person's deep, unacknowledged hunger decentres him and clouds his thinking. Over prolonged periods, simply being around emotionally undernourished people triggers an intense desire for sweet foods such as chocolate, soft drinks, pastries and sugary breakfast cereals. These are foods that Julius happily ignores when he's alone. When charged up on sugary foods, he makes poor decisions and experiences limited patience and concentration for delicate tasks.

Pia's particular sensitivity is also dietary. Her digestive system is intolerant to a range of cuisines and some food groups even trigger allergic reactions such as skin rashes, tightness in her throat and physical exhaustion. Over the years, she has learned to read the labels of all foodstuffs to avoid dairy products, chillies, garlic and certain grains. It makes dining out challenging. However, it's still better for her than experiencing difficulty breathing, physical and mental fatigue or digestive issues after eating these foods.

Angela's son Tyson is hyper-sensitive to sounds, so a trip out shopping requires noise-cancelling headphones. She keeps a set in the car, another pair in the house and a third set in his backpack. Even at school, he wears small, foam ear inserts that reduce noise levels while still enabling him to hear people around him in the classroom. This allows Tyson to concentrate without becoming overwhelmed. Different personal sensitivities require unique solutions, especially when living in a busy city or with limited dietary options.

PERSONAL, EMOTIONAL AND SPIRITUAL BOUNDARIES

Sensitivity to the emotions of others is sometimes caused by poor personal boundaries. Your skin is a physical boundary, marking where your actual body ends and the world around you begins. In a home, windows, doors and curtains are all boundaries. A locked door prevents entry, while a closed blind restricts vision from outside the home.

Acknowledging emotional perimeters includes not asking questions that might offend someone, or prying into the lives of others. It can mean not assuming that personal plans involving other people are okay with them without first enquiring.

When Ted purchased a skydive for his wife Renita, he didn't think to enquire if she would be open to the experience. He didn't want to spoil the surprise.

"I'm afraid of heights," she said flatly when he explained the adventure ahead for her as they drove to the airfield.

Respecting mental limits includes not reading someone's diary, agreeing to disagree with others without denigrating them and crediting other people for their ideas when using them in public.

Respecting spiritual boundaries includes not trespassing in the energy fields of others without permission, not using magic, spells or other distance methods to control the health, wellbeing or actions of others and not intuitively asking questions of friends or strangers in meditation without their express permission. Powerless people sometimes find magic appealing. Giving scant thought to the long-term consequences of such prying actions doesn't prevent the likely negative outcomes for the person recklessly traversing the parameters of others. If you read another person's diary, be prepared to be mentioned in disparaging tones. If using magic to control others, don't be surprised if people begin to use it against you.

When people are violent, they breach the physical boundaries of others. When an individual torments another through words, this often breaches emotional and mental limits or expectations of safety. If prolonged, this destructive behaviour can also injure the recipient spiritually. When magic is used to control another person negatively, it violates physical, emotional, mental and spiritual boundaries, potentially derailing that individual's life.

Sadly, when people hurt or bully others, they have often been oppressed themselves. Unaddressed past injuries are often passed on to others, spreading the suffering without resolving it. This is why it's essential to scan over the childhood years of your clients to glimpse any raw, unresolved incidents that have shaped their lives. It's difficult to blame someone for poor behaviour when the causes of their internal anguish are obvious.

Extending beyond your physical frame (or boundary), are your emotional body, mental form and several spiritual bodies. These can radiate far outside the physical form. Sometimes when demonstrating psychic protection in courses, I'll ask a volunteer to close their eyes and spiritually protect themself to the best of their ability. When this is confirmed, I mentally scan them for any weaknesses.

If none are immediately apparent, I produce a box of matches, open it and rearrange the matches. The volunteer's eyes remain closed but they usually become curious. While listening intently to decipher what I'm doing, they unconsciously send out a small, psychic energy cord towards the matchbox. I then follow that cord and slip into their energy field, where I begin describing their physical health, their friends and family members. This is simply a demonstration of how a determined person can often circumvent everyday psychic protection.

Other activities that expand a person's emotional and spiritual energy bodies include drinking alcohol or taking recreational drugs. This is why some shy individuals enjoy the effect of drugs or alcohol; they can help them feel comfortable with strangers. Unfamiliar people feel more comfortable to them because they are effectively inside the other person's expanded energy field. When others are inside your energy field, it's easy to be affected by their actions and any residual negative energy. Like catering to house guests, you'll need to clean up after they leave.

EXTENDED SPIRITUAL AND EMOTIONAL BODIES

In psychic development classes, it's not uncommon to have one or more students with extended spiritual and emotional bodies. These energy spheres can fill a room or a whole house and often haven't been acknowledged by the owner. When these individuals arrive for a course, fellow students usually sit within their energy fields for the whole day.

By focusing awareness on personal boundaries at the beginning of each of the three days in a course, everyone in the room becomes more conscious of energy fields and of anyone else whose spiritual or emotional body is filling the room. It's essential to address this early on because it affects every student when they are attempting intuitive reading exercises.

In one group exercise, where the goal was to spontaneously

describe the interior of a volunteer's home, students were struggling to be accurate when describing David's apartment. Instead, two participants accurately pinpointed another student Shelley's living room, her small dog, her fireplace and her new dishwasher. To illustrate how this was because they were sitting in Shelley's expanded aura, I asked Shelley to step out of the room for a few minutes to gauge the accuracy levels. They rose immediately, as students were no longer attempting to tune out interference.

When Dianne sat down on the first day of a course, it was apparent that her aura was wide open. I felt enveloped by her emotions, as if I was a guest in her territory. She was a warm-hearted, sensitive woman, so it was important to address her expanded field without judgement. When these fields are wide open, a person can be easily drained by others because nearby people are effectively inside her aura. Dianne confirmed that she was often drained in gatherings. Any group event, including dining in a crowded café, attending a church service, watching a school sports game or standing in line at a supermarket can become an ordeal, as the person is burdened by all of the fears, worries, hopes and resentments of surrounding people. This can limit avenues for socialising unless gatherings are restricted to fewer than five people at once.

I demonstrated a few simple boundary tests and students paired off to practise. I encouraged Dianne and several others to venture outside, where they might be away from the energy fields of other students. When we sat together after the practice sessions, I asked if everyone was aware of their own energetic boundaries and they nodded. I then enquired if anyone felt that they were inside the aura of any other students in the room. Everyone mentioned Dianne.

I then asked Dianne if she would be willing to demonstrate a technique to contract emotional, mental and spiritual boundaries.

After Dianne had learned to contract her energy field, I demonstrated with two other volunteers so that she could observe the process. For the rest of that course every few hours, I heard someone say, "Dianne, you're doing it again. I'm trying to focus here." Dianne laughed and consciously contracted her aura again. If someone's aura is naturally expanded, it can require repeated practice of the contraction process until the cause of the expansion is identified and resolved. Causes of an expanded aura might include past trauma, physical accidents or injuries, serious surgery and exploring psychic realms without proper protection. Over the years, I've trained myself not to be curious about strangers in public, to avoid silently stepping into their auras and unconsciously collecting their dross.

When people have had expanded auras for many years, that state is familiar to them. Contracting it again requires training and vigilance. By consciously strengthening physical, emotional, mental and spiritual boundaries, it's possible to reduce awareness of the desires, fears and emotions of people in home or work environments. This hyper-awareness can be caused by a lack of training around personal limits as a child or having endured a parent, teacher or family member who repeatedly invaded or violated personal boundaries. If this is the case, a counsellor, coach or therapist might assist with identifying and solidifying personal borders, essentially strengthening the individual's physical and emotional skin.

When training psychics to respect the boundaries of others, I say, "Every time you look into a window, you have to clean it. Then you have to cleanse yourself." I remind them that others have the right to keep secrets and that searching into the lives of friends and strangers without invitation is trespassing. Intuitive or spiritual trespass brings its own unwanted burdens and karmic implications. Maintaining strong personal boundaries improves focus and reduces energy loss to other people.

CONTRACTING THE ENERGY FIELD

We contract our boundaries swiftly and instinctively when we walk through a large spider web at night. Unable to determine if the spider is still in the newly broken web or clinging to our hair or clothing, we often take a quick breath and contract our energy fields for protection. Of course, this won't shield us if an angry, newly homeless spider is hanging on to our clothing but this is simply a natural human response.

In Australia, where house spiders can grow to the size of your hand, people become adept at walking into a room and sensing a spider before they see it. Perhaps self-preservation is nature's way of improving personal intuition. Huntsman spiders are not a serious threat to life but they can shock people.

My sister, who lives in the bush, assures me that it's a similar experience with snakes. If she's gardening and thinks of a snake, she becomes much more open to the possibility of encountering one of these reptiles while gardening. It's almost as if they are announcing their presence. As soon as she thinks of snakes, she becomes automatically more vigilant. This hyper-awareness is usually rewarded with a snake sighting sometime during that day.

A less stressful but equally effective response occurs when a person sees an unwanted ex-partner at a club, in a crowded market or at a celebration. The reaction is often to withdraw the personal energy field tightly around the physical body, to seem invisible and less likely to be confronted. It's simply an attempt to fade to grey, as one might if approaching someone to whom they owed an unpaid debt.

UNUSUALLY SENSITIVE PEOPLE

Naturally intuitive individuals are often more sensitive to foods, light, sounds and environmental changes. Sometimes they are hypersensitive to one or more of these. This restricts the number of situations where they feel comfortable until they adapt or learn how to 'turn down' the volume on their sensitivities. If they don't deliberately strengthen personal boundaries, they'll usually retreat from social situations, crowded work environments and busy shopping centres, preferring to live alone, work from home and shop online.

People who are unusually sensitive to surrounding sounds often have a well-developed sense of smell. Foods that they are intolerant to can be identified through careful medical testing. They can become easily overwhelmed by strong perfumes, aftershaves and scents from pungent flowers, pets and even new furniture.

The sense of smell is often linked with memories from past people, friendships and situations. This can influence fragrance-sensitive individuals when meeting new people who are wearing perfumes that remind them of past friends or colleagues. In the early 1990s, many of my female clients arrived for readings wearing a popular perfume that smelled like dust to me. I felt as though I had placed my face into a vacuum cleaner dirt bag for an hour at the end of each session. I was very glad when that particular scent became less popular.

Individuals with heightened sensitivity to others are often keenly aware of criticism or intolerance from surrounding people. Some might describe this as being thin-skinned. As the skin is the layer of us that separates what is outside of us from what's within, it has to work harder at separating sensitive people from the physical and emotional worlds around them.

It's possible that as children, a parent, teacher or guardian might have ignored their personal attempts to set limits, to the point where they have no real boundaries between themselves and the rest of the world. Unable to filter out what originates from outside the physical body, the sensitive person feels everything acutely, as though it is happening within them. This process makes them feel fuzzy-headed or exhausted if they spend even a short time in a crowd of people. A few hours spent in shopping centres, bars or at sports events can leave them feeling shattered. Instead of avoiding all contact with people, they can reinforce personal perimeters and learn to turn down their sensitivity when required.

It's important to strengthen personal limits while improving intuition, to avoid crossing the boundaries of others. Boundary crossing occurs when someone provides intuitive information without invitation, such as giving predictions to people who didn't request or want them. It is a form of trespassing, as it involves peering into the lives of others without invitation. I've had students try to justify this behaviour by insisting that they were only trying to help. I wonder who they were actually assisting by spying. This type of invasive habit is usually a red flag, the result of unhealed past trauma that shattered personal borders. It's often ego, centred on a desire to impress others with personal psychic abilities. It's usually a sign of a beginner or someone who has poor personal boundaries.

Controlling sensitivity involves being aware of your current surroundings and then reducing your auric energy field. With practice, it's easy to achieve this. Children often display this expanded energy because they haven't yet learned how to energetically close themselves down. Any parent of a three-year-old knows the sense of emptiness in the home when that child is away at kindergarten or visiting a friend. The house becomes more restful and quieter and sometimes it can feel hollow without the child's amplified presence.

ENERGY AWARENESS EXERCISE

In courses, I usually invite someone with an expanded energy field to join me in an energy awareness exercise. We stand facing each other from opposite corners of the room. I ask this person to simply be aware of their physical body. I then request that they tell me when they sense any discomfort physically as I slowly walk towards them. We maintain eye contact until they eventually stop me. Occasionally, they don't stop me until we are almost touching noses.

During this exercise, I observe this individual carefully, searching for minute signs of discomfort. These might include a long, slow blink, holding the breath, a slight movement suggesting a desire to turn and walk away, smiling or curling the fingers. I also notice when I'm entering each layer of that person's energy field.

After the exercise, we discuss any uneasiness they experienced. It is important to be aware of any part of the body that signals discomfort. Tightness in the throat, the chest or the jaw might be a warning sign that something is not quite right. Paying attention to the physical body alerts people to imminent danger or changing circumstances. It's a natural, human, protective mechanism.

Some students discover that different parts of the physical body tighten up to signal separate threats or boundaries being crossed. Tina noticed that when her throat tightened, she had difficulty setting limits. In response, she learned to step back from any surrounding person or situation when this happened. It helped her to gain strength and notice what triggered that particular response within. In contrast, when her belly felt disturbed, it was a sign that someone around her had psychically corded her for energy. This occurs when a person's innate desires unconsciously form invisible psychic cords, through which they drain another person's spiritual energy and vitality.

Tina soon recognised who spent time with her when they needed energy and not necessarily because they enjoyed her company.

It's difficult to avoid particular foods, sounds and people, especially when living and working in a city. For individuals who are sensitive to specific nutrients and food additives, it's possible to prepare meals from scratch or find a few suitable cafés or bakeries.

Sensitivity to sound sometimes requires a home in a quiet suburb, a dead-end street or a property on the outskirts of a city, surrounded by nature. It might also rule out apartment living, sharing a rental house with many co-tenants or residing close to nightlife but peace is usually worth pursuing. The benefits include more restful sleep at night, deeper meditations and improved concentration when reading, working or studying.

For individuals living in crowded suburbs or apartment buildings, foam earplugs worn at night can reduce disturbance during sleep and indoor fountains can distract the ear from surrounding sounds. Soft, soothing music can also divert attention from a neighbour's constantly barking dogs. If music becomes distracting, a soothing recording of waves breaking on shore can help.

With city life, focusing on survival and earning an income can soon become more important than avoiding spiritually empty people. Carefully choosing friends and a partner who also pursue spiritual nourishment is a bonus. Additional personal replenishment—such as regular ocean swimming, yoga sessions or meditation—might be necessary to offset the effects of living and working with materialistic people who only believe what they can see or touch.

BEING CENTRED IN THE PRESENT

When not centred in the current moment, it sometimes helps to retrace your steps back to the last time you were truly present. If it was several hours or even a few days ago, the last person, place or thing you'll remember clearly is the time you were actually present. When this occurs, take a moment to notice what took you away from your surroundings. Was it a thought or a conversation? Perhaps it was a comment or a criticism from someone? It might have been a smell, such as a perfume or a familiar food recalled from childhood.

By noticing what takes you away from the here and now, it becomes clearer when particular people, situations or circumstances repeatedly trigger a retreat from your surroundings. All power lies in the immediate moment. When someone is not alive to the opportunities available in each unique moment, possibilities are usually squandered, meaning that you overlook chances to shape or reshape your destiny.

When Olaf consulted me to stop smoking cigarettes, he was surprised that I didn't tell him how bad they might be for his health or what he might be doing to his children by smoking around them. Instead, I invited him outside to watch the last of the sun's rays disappear behind some tall, silver-trunked gum trees.

I suggested that he light a cigarette and be absolutely aware through each moment — from reaching for the box to opening the top, to selecting one of the five cigarettes in the box and closing the lip. I requested that he become acutely mindful of the feel of the box and the sensation of the cigarette in his fingers. Then I asked him to describe what the lighter felt like in his hands. It was a small, deep blue, oval-shaped cylinder and it took three attempts to create a flame to light the cigarette.

I encouraged him to describe the first inward breath, the taste of the smoke in his mouth and the growing ash on the tip as it burned down to the filter. He outlined every single part of the process in detail, right down to the aftertaste in his mouth after he had extinguished his cigarette. I suggested that he sniff his fingers and describe the smell, then lick his lips and explain the taste and later to smell his jacket and do the same.

By helping Olaf to be present while smoking, he could decide whether he enjoyed the process and why. He could also explain what he disliked and why. By participating in this activity, Olaf discovered that he detested the taste of smoke in his mouth. He then decided that one of his objectives was to maintain a fresh taste in his mouth all day.

Beyond this new awareness of what Olaf disliked about smoking, we were able to find a replacement for lighting up that relaxed him and was as portable as smoking. Inhaling the smoke from cigarettes was once a very convenient and instant way for him to relax. In recent times however, it had become a routine where he was forced to leave the office, apartment or restaurant and stand outside in all types of inclement weather until he finished his cigarette.

On long-haul flights, it's difficult to step outside for a quick drag; nor can occupants of a 21st-floor apartment that doesn't have a balcony. There is now a range of more convenient relaxation techniques than smoking, including breathing exercises, meditations or asking for the light. (See Chapters 11 and 27 for more information about accessing spiritual light.)

SIMPLE BREATHING EXERCISE

Here is a simple breathing exercise that you can do in only a few minutes:

1. Take a long slow, inward breath while mentally counting from one to four.

2. Now, hold this breath while continuing to count from five to eight.
3. Release this breath while counting slowly from one to four.
4. Don't breathe in while counting from five to eight. Then repeat the process from the start as many times as you need.

By focusing on counting while breathing, it's possible to become more centred in the present and gradually more relaxed, without the negative results of smoking. When focused in the moment, you experience increased awareness of your current surroundings. Sometimes, instead of improving our home or work conditions, it's easier to simply ignore them. If the immediate environment is enhanced instead of disregarded, it can become a more rewarding place to be. This might require a more supportive office chair, increased light from the addition of a floor lamp, a fountain outside your home office window to divert attention from passing traffic, or a scented candle to offset a co-worker's garlic-chilli lunch.

10.
DIET AFFECTS INTUITION

As a person increases their sensitivity to information and the energy fields of others, that individual gradually becomes more subtly aware of surrounding sounds, fragrances and foods. It's important to notice how particular meals affect the physical body. When keeping an intuitive diary of predictions, it is valuable to record personal diet as well as energy levels.

For some individuals, avoidance of sugar is paramount in the intuitive development process, as they become less centred or aware after consuming sweeteners in various forms. Although an initial energy rush can make us feel focused and motivated, 90 to 120 minutes later, there is often a crash point when personal blood sugar levels plummet. At this time, a person might reach for more sweet foods or become tired, listless and less effective until the body restores its natural equilibrium. Some people notice that if their day begins with a range of sweetened foods, they can experience several highs and lows before sunset. If the first meal of the day contains only natural substances such as fruit (fructose), the person is less susceptible to the rollercoaster of dietary cravings. For others, the consumption of dairy products or red meat can influence personal awareness and accuracy. Everyone is unique in discovering which, if any, foods negatively influence their intuitive awareness.

For people wanting to reach great spiritual heights in meditation, the consumption of garlic is best avoided as it tends to limit clear spiritual awareness. It's possible to enjoy deep, reflective periods after eating garlic but it's difficult to receive accurate spiritual insights during introspection for several days after consumption.

When Ellyn began private lessons in psychic development, she explained that despite regular meditation practice, she was unable to inwardly "see" her guides or psychic cords. At first, I assumed that she required a different meditation technique. When that didn't help, we explored external and internal distractions that might be limiting her success.

Despite closing the door to her study before meditation to keep her cat out, playing relaxing music during these periods and meditating at different times of the day, Ellyn still struggled with the process. Then I asked her to talk me through every action she took from waking up until she sat down to meditate. Her start to the day included drinking a cup of herbal tea with a healthy breakfast but then she mentioned in passing that she ate a chocolate bar with her morning tea directly before meditation.

I suggested that she avoid the chocolate bar or eat it after meditation, to gauge any difference in the meditation process. Also, that she avoid chocolate, tea or coffee on the day of her next lesson, to allow me to notice any difference. The following week, Ellyn shared that her meditations on the days she didn't eat chocolate were slightly better. She seemed more focused during her lesson and, although this was an improvement, it wasn't the breakthrough that she was hoping for.

I asked her to tell me exactly what she had eaten for breakfast on the days she went without chocolate before meditation. She mentioned whole-wheat toast and I probed to see what she spread on it. It was butter and jam, so I requested that she avoid these on the no-chocolate days to see if her focus and meditation results improved.

During her next lesson, Ellyn enthusiastically explained how she had seen more than ever before during meditations after changing her toast spread to avocado topped with sliced tomato and cracked pepper. With a few more steps of elimination and reintroduction, we established that a mild intolerance to dairy reduced Ellyn's intuitive clarity and focus for hours after consumption. As she intentionally decreased her dairy intake over the next few months, Ellyn's meditations sharpened and she was able to see her higher self, as well as scan her pets for health issues.

The obvious culprits in limiting intuitive awareness for all of us include alcohol, smoking, too much junk food and some prescribed medications. Obviously, it makes sense to consult a doctor or a qualified health practitioner before withdrawing from any medicines and remember that not all medications influence awareness. Temporary elimination of a food and then reintroduction after a short period can help to identify what, if any, foods lower personal sensitivity. This is only effective if everything else in your personal diet and life remains the same during these test periods.

Because intuitive sensitivity requires a delicate balance of mind and body, seemingly insignificant foods, sounds, smells and worries can upset this balance, resulting in poor meditations with unreliable results. During psychic development courses, I closely monitor the physical energy and concentration levels of students throughout the day. Often, they return from lunch with poor attention for the rest of the day. When this occurs, they have effectively lost half a day because they are unlikely to remember anything that they were not mentally present for during the learning sessions.

Several years ago, I ran a weekend psychic development course interstate where this post-lunch stupor was extreme. These two-day intensive courses were packed with theory, demonstrations, games and exercises to help students explore what worked for them.

When Nancy returned from lunch on the second day, her auric energy field was fuzzy. It had been an almost-even line around her physical body throughout the morning but was suddenly jagged and uneven, especially around her head.

I asked her if she had found a suitable café for lunch and what she had chosen to eat, wondering if she was energetically imbalanced due to her food intake. She mentioned that she had enjoyed the house special. This turned out to be roast lamb with vegetables and a glass of red wine. I didn't need to enquire any further, as a glass of wine was enough to dull her sensitivity. She had forgotten my request that all students avoid alcohol for the duration of the course. Consequently, she found that none of the intuitive exercises she attempted that afternoon were successful. Her intuitive skills before and after lunch were in sharp contrast. Developing intuition is challenging enough without adding distractions to the process.

Clear, powerful meditative experiences are rare enough, so discovering what negatively influences personal attention or mental equilibrium is essential for increasing intuitive success. A person needs to be centred, calm and mentally still to glean clear insight in meditation, especially when tracing a thread of information to retrieve more details.

It's easy to notice how diet affects concentration when trying to read a story or complete a complex project. If our focus on everyday tasks is affected by food or drink recently ingested, our sensitivity to more subtle energies is often disturbed too.

Just as young children become restless and less coordinated after processed foods and sugary drinks (think red cordial or fizzy drinks), adults are also influenced by their daily diet. This was clearly apparent at a five-year-old's birthday party I attended with my young son many years ago. The country homestead was surrounded by rolling lawns, allowing the children plenty of space to run and play. A dozen kids played cricket in the warm sun while adults reclined in the shade of the veranda. Because the birthday boy was intolerant to a range of foods, a variety of homemade, naturally sweetened foods were crowded onto tables inside.

There was plenty of laugher, enthusiasm and harmony, until 4 pm when the birthday cake and sweets arrived. Within 30 minutes, one child had walked into the thin edge of a door, another had fallen off the veranda and two more were crying after being bruised during a rough game. As the sugar hit, they became more enthusiastic and less coordinated, hurting themselves and others. Within an hour, half a dozen children were bundled into cars and taken home crying. Kids that had played happily together for hours began fighting and it looked like a children's version of closing time at a rough, inner-city bar.

"Whose idea was the chocolate cake?" I overheard one parent growl as she steered her tearful child towards the car.

11. FOUR APPROACHES TO INTUITIVE READING

There are four basic techniques for intuitive reading that suit different circumstances. With practice, most people specialise in one method but can also use others when required.

METHOD 1: ALLOWING INFORMATION TO REACH YOUR CONSCIOUS MIND

This method allows information in your immediate environment to filter into your conscious mind. It sounds deceptively simple. However, getting a busy mind out of the way requires patience and persistence. When you've stilled your mind and can notice new information steadily arriving, there's plenty of it to be received. Unconsciously, many people already sense emotions and surrounding energy within their immediate environments. They sometimes don't know this because often this data does not reach the conscious mind. It can get blocked in its path to conscious awareness or lost beneath everyday distractions that absorb the person's mental focus.

Sometimes we react to new information without noticing. I introduced a friend, Jason, to a colleague one afternoon. Directly after

Jason shook Cooper's hand, he wiped his own hand on his chef's apron. This unconscious reaction suggested that he immediately took a dislike to Cooper. When I mentioned it later, Jason had no memory of doing this but concurred with my assessment of the meeting; he didn't like my colleague.

When meeting someone new, the subconscious mind receives vast amounts of information about that particular person. Being self-conscious at first meeting filters out most of this information because you place more attention on yourself than the other person. It's not necessary to focus carefully or intently on everything that is said. Instead, acknowledge some signature signs, such as how information is presented, the initial feeling of connection and how much attention the other person is devoting to the interaction to gain insight. If someone who is being introduced is present and attentive, the meeting is likely to be more memorable because emotional and mental connection relies on people being aware and present in the moment.

Everyone knows the feeling of standing together in conversation with someone at a gathering while that person scans the room for someone else to talk to. At a party recently, I stood on a veranda talking with a well-dressed woman named Clara while dozens of people gathered around a brilliantly lit swimming pool beneath us, laughing and talking. Strings of coloured lanterns were draped across trees as waiters moved through the throng with platters of savoury pastries, feeding everyone. As conversation flowed between us, I noticed Clara scanning the crowd, deciding where to locate herself next. Sensing that she was restless, I excused myself to refresh my drink and she immediately moved on.

"I see that you've met Clara then," said my friend Tony as I surveyed a table of sweet foods. "She's in politics," he said drily.

"That makes sense. Working late tonight, then?" I quipped.

When someone gives you minimal attention, it can indicate that they don't value what's being provided or that the conversation is a warm-up for a better interaction elsewhere. Afterwards, you're likely to forget the experience rapidly or only recall it as a negative interaction. It can be difficult to remain present and emotionally available for someone who is distracted or who wants to be somewhere else.

However, if two people begin a conversation that provides a positive experience through shared interests or mutual respect, future meetings are likely to be more warmly pursued. Being vulnerable and risking disappointment are important parts of a more authentic social experience. This exposure can be enhanced by allowing unconscious information to reach your conscious mind.

Many years ago, I met a photographer three times in five weeks for publicity shots. The first time, Karin arrived at my front door to photograph me for a magazine. As a freelancer, she was hired by a range of magazines and travelled in a car loaded with equipment.

The first meeting was straightforward. She asked me a few questions about the feature story the magazine was running and took some shots, packed up and left.

Two weeks later, she was back, representing a different magazine. This time I offered her coffee and biscuits. It can't be easy travelling around all day. We had a brief conversation while she unpacked. Three weeks later, I opened the door and there she was, with a smile.

"It's me again," she said, clutching a duffle bag in one hand and a camera bag over her shoulder.

"White with two sugars," I said, flinging the door open and beckoning her to enter. This time she seemed tired and slightly brittle and she berated herself when she couldn't find a clamp. I made coffee while she unpacked her equipment.

"How are we going to do something different?" she asked, sighing as she dropped onto the sofa.

"You could always photograph the back of my head," I quipped cheekily but there was no reaction. She seemed unavailable, preoccupied.

Soon the process was proceeding. I held up a book in a few shots and a porcelain hand in a few more.

"Which is your best side?" she asked as she scrolled through the recent images.

"I don't know," I replied.

"Sure you don't," she snapped, assuming I was fishing for compliments. Encountering the shocked look on my face, she stopped abruptly and apologised.

"I've just had some bad news," she said. "I should have gone straight home after the last phone call but the editor needs these photos tonight." She explained that a vet had just told her that her ageing dog Rory needed surgery and might not survive it. Holding back tears, she retrieved her phone and showed me some images of her dog.

Looking back on this interaction, if I hadn't noticed that she seemed distracted, I might have responded tersely with a raised eyebrow before abruptly announcing that the shoot was finished and she would have to work with the images she already had. However, sensing that she was tired and fragile that day saved me from rebuking her rudeness. Instead, her tearful conversation began a long friendship. Having positive interactions during the previous visits also helped.

With experience, receiving information within your immediate vicinity becomes easier so that events outside the room, the street, or the city are not simultaneously crowding into your mind. By establishing a two-or-three-metre perimeter, it's possible to read for a stranger who is sitting in the room while remaining unaware of the events in the rest of the building. This technique requires well-developed personal focus.

The success of this method relies on a strong boundary being established and enforced so that details being received are focused solely on the person being read. Form an initial limit by mentally deciding where to devote your attention. A mother of a young baby usually does this regularly if the child is asleep in another room. She is capable of paying attention to circumstances in her immediate environment while listening for any sounds that suggest her child is awake. In a personal reading, a firm boundary can be established using white light.

Establishing a Boundary with White Light

1. Begin by requesting protection.
2. Take a moment to mentally ask for the light.
3. Take a deep breath and simultaneously draw as much light into your body as possible (down through your crown).
4. Breathe out while forcing this white light out through your brow chakra (or energy centre) and visualise it forming a ball around you. Above ground, it seems like a dome but it is essential that it

covers beneath you for full protection.
5. Expand that light to include the person you're reading for, or simply use this white light as a buffer to filter fear, dross or negativity.

If a stronger boundary is required, you can use a line of sea salt around the room, encircling the reader and the guest. Alternatively, use four bowls of water containing sea salt (a large cup of salt in each bowl) placed in the corners of the room. This is a more subtle method that is less likely to conjure thoughts of ritual sacrifice in the minds of visitors. Stepping into a visible circle of sea salt on the floor could make some people nervous. The client might hastily say, "I've just remembered something that I urgently have to do" (i.e., get out of here) while rushing towards the door.

I keep a large glass bowl of salt water in the office to absorb negative emotions so that each person arrives at an energetically clean room. By changing the water and salt regularly, the room remains neutral. If my office overlooked the ocean, I'd simply open a window to achieve the same effect.

The white light process establishes a perimeter between what you are doing (inside the circle) and the rest of the world. This is a spiritual boundary but there are already other, more physical borders in place before meditating or reading for another person.

- Close the door to the room to avoid interruptions from children or pets. This is a physical line of demarcation.
- Turn off your phone. This is another boundary; it sends a message to callers that you are not available right now.
- If you have another client directly after this one, you would have previously agreed on a start time for the next session. This is a time boundary.

Then, gradually still your mind and sort through the information that is arriving, moment by moment, to determine what is relevant to yourself or the client. With more experience, you can progressively open your awareness to receive additional information. Doing this suddenly can be overwhelming, so it's important to be patient with the process. Think of it like standing at the edge of a lake and reaching in with cupped hands to taste some fresh, cool water instead of plunging directly into the cold depths.

Gradually, it's possible to form stronger boundaries, an essential part of intuitive development. This is especially important for people who are extremely sensitive to their immediate surroundings. (See also Chapter 9 'Strategies for Sensitivity'.)

METHOD 2: TRACING INFORMATION THREADS

The second technique for intuitive reading involves moving from a macro to a micro approach, or from the big picture to a more detailed perspective. This involves stilling the mind while searching for a single thread of information. Once a suitable stream is found, it is necessary to trace that strand to its origin to explore an issue in more detail. It's not a difficult technique but it does require practice. (For more information, please refer to Chapter 22 'Tracing threads of information' and Chapter 23 'Working backwards from the future'.)

If you already read for clients, you might ask each person if they'd like an additional five minutes of a new method you are trialling, at the end of each reading. This is not possible if there is another client waiting for a session but it can be done with the client immediately before lunch and with the last person of the day.

This process usually suits specific questions. When a recent client asked about her eldest daughter, I asked her for the girl's name and age. Jasmine was nine years old. Her name gave me something to search for. I had several options for finding the first thread of information.

- I could search for a psychic energy cord from the mother's belly that would have been established before birth, trace along the cord to Jasmine and then describe her physical appearance to ensure I had located the right child.

- It was possible to mentally ask for Jasmine until I could see her clearly in my mind's eye.
- A third option involved mentally scanning Jasmine's home to see her family and then selecting the child who appears to be nine years of age.

It's necessary to describe the physical appearance and character traits of the person to confirm you're not giving information about another child in the family. In this reading, I described Jasmine as having a large, oval-shaped face, blonde hair and big blue eyes. She was a bit of a princess but also sensible and independent.

Once I have agreement from the client that I have described the right person, it's possible to scan back several years or forward throughout that person's life. I asked if Jasmine had lost a close friend when she was seven years of age. I saw a good friend moving away from Jasmine's school as her family was relocating. It had taken Jasmine almost a year to accept the loss of their solid friendship.

This technique is like shining a torch into the dark. Whatever is illuminated by the thin beam can be described. The weakness of this method is that specific details don't always make sense without context. If I had glimpsed Jasmine dreading her day ahead, it would be easy to assume that she was an anxious child. By broadening my focus to include her whole day or her week ahead, I might discover that she is worried about an exam or an impending visit to the dentist.

In another reading, Emma sat hunched over the table as she selected cards while asking about her health. First, I explained to her that I was not medically trained and could not provide a diagnosis. I suggested that she consult a medical doctor or health specialist if she had any concerns about her wellbeing. I then used this method to scan down through her body, beginning with the head and then the neck and throat down to the feet. My attention was immediately drawn to the upper neck. There was tension in and around the third vertebrae from the top. Without any conscious analysis, I knew that it was an old injury from a car crash.

"I see some tension in the upper neck and it seems like it is the result of a sudden physical shock many years ago. Did you suffer a neck injury a long time ago?" I asked Emma. She explained that she had been in a car accident in her early 20s and had experienced ongoing neck pain in the months following the unexpected collision.

Moving my awareness down slowly to the throat, I noticed a thin trace of a chemical that lined her throat, stomach and intestines. It was due to something she drank regularly and this synthetic substance was preventing a range of nutrients from reaching her bloodstream. Instead of mentioning this and having her dismiss it as inaccurate, I asked a few questions.

"Do you drink coffee or tea regularly?" I asked.

"Yes, coffee."

"Do you have it white?"

"No. Black with a dash of milk," she replied, making me slightly confused. On closer examination, milk wasn't causing this issue.

"Do you have sugar or an artificial sweetener with it?"

"No."

"I'm seeing the regular intake of some type of artificial sweetener."

"No. I don't have sweetened coffee. Oh, wait a minute. I have a hot chocolate every day but that doesn't contain sugar."

"Is it sweet?"

"Yes."

"What sort of sweetener does it use? I ask this because cocoa or powdered chocolate is slightly bitter and both need a sweetener to make them palatable."

"I guess it uses an artificial sweetener," she said, nodding.

"Can you switch to a hot chocolate that uses sugar or make one from scratch using honey as a sweetener? I think that your physical energy levels might improve after you stop consuming the chemical that is lining your intestines."

I then mentally scanned her lungs. They seemed tired and slightly grey, suggesting that she was once a smoker but hadn't smoked lately. Again, I posed this as a question.

"I'm scanning your lungs now. Do you smoke?"

"No."

"Did you smoke in the past?"

"Yes. I gave up almost ten years ago."

"How long did you smoke before that?"

"Almost 20 years."

"Your lungs look fine but show signs of past stress, possibly from smoking."

Using this method, I then examined the organs, the bloodstream, her hands for arthritis indication and her legs for signs of mobility issues. Her thighs and calf muscles were strong, suggesting that she walked long distances regularly as a child. She explained that she walked to and from school each day, a five-kilometre round trip.

It's possible to mentally scan a person's health forwards in time five or ten years and scan the body again at a particular age. Recently, when I scanned someone's body five years ahead, I noticed that her feet were red, her skin was dry and flaking and her toes looked slightly red and swollen. This might be a symptom of the effects of diabetes, so I suggested that she see her doctor for tests.

With some health issues, early intervention, changing diet or increasing physical exercise can prevent ill health or delay the onset of problems. Every decision, action or reaction by an individual determines events ahead in that person's life. Occasionally, people need to be encouraged to maintain physical fitness and wellbeing. At other times, it's necessary to urge them to consult a specialist to avoid serious health issues. This needs to be done without alarming clients but clearly enough to motivate them to actively focus on their physical health.

METHOD 3: CONTACTING SPIRITUAL GUIDES

The third approach to information retrieval is to ask your spirit guides to provide more insights about a topic, person or situation. Meditating to contact guides can be time consuming. With practice, it's possible to access guides by simply asking inwardly. However, results using this method can be less accurate, especially if you're uncentred when requesting information.

Guides are a powerful source of information for personal development. They can help reveal individual blind spots, prejudices or negative patterns and also explain how these were formed in early life. If it is necessary for you to meditate to still your mind when contacting guides, this may not be an effective method for face-to-face readings with clients. It might work well on the phone but the reader having closed eyes for the duration of a personal reading can be disconcerting for people.

Sometimes when inexperienced individuals attempt to contact guides, they end up contacting their higher selves but if the information received is accurate and helpful, it doesn't matter. Essentially, guides are beings in spirit, between human lives, who can advise people on their choices and consequences, whereas the higher self is the spiritually developed self. It's the part of us that shares our history and future and is invested in helping us make decisions for our highest benefit.

Imagine watching a film while seated next to your higher self. Your spiritual self has already seen the whole film and knows the ending. Consequently, it doesn't stress when events in the film turn bad and the outcome suddenly looks bleak. Being aware of life's bigger picture, your higher self can guide you towards a safe and rewarding outcome. If you're unsure about what is most important in a particular moment, simply ask, "What do I most need to know right now?"

In a recent reading, Lillian seemed exhausted. She had the appearance of a 70-year-old woman but she was only 38. She was unsteady on her feet when she walked in and seemed frail and depleted. Recovering from recent surgery, she explained that her reserves of energy had been fading for almost two years. She was struggling to stay awake through the session and her concentration was intermittent at best. She hadn't slept properly for two weeks and had barely eaten in the past three days. Sensing that this was more than the result of physical illness, I asked her permission to meditate briefly and contact my guides for an effective course of action to restore her vitality.

I closed my eyes and entered a light meditation to be told by my guides that Lillian had given up on life. After years of struggling to maintain her retail clothing business while juggling her home and caring for her ageing mother, she had lost faith that life might offer her joy or lasting fulfilment. She had been living alone for 15 years and her sole happiness was found in running her shop. When the economy dipped, her business faltered and didn't recover.

Because she had essentially given up on life, Lillian no longer meditated, rarely exercised or socialised and gradually turned away from all of her sources of emotional and spiritual nourishment. It was as though the light no longer reached her. She was 'running on empty'.

My guides explained that intricate or complicated techniques for restoring her balance were likely to be forgotten before she left the room, so it was imperative that I provide simple methods with baby steps. I gave her a pen and paper and requested that she list my suggestions for later reference.

I asked her to spend five to ten minutes a day sitting or standing in the morning sun. It was a cold winter but Sydney winters have plenty of sunny days that can be enjoyed if you're in a protected corner of a garden.

I suggested that she consciously allow nourishing food, the good intentions of friends or staff and her comfortable home to reach her in her heart. It was important that she focus on gratitude to notice the bounty around her. I asked for the light to reach and nourish her before encouraging Lillian to request the same thing for herself. Asking for the light to reach another person is similar to praying for someone's wellbeing. It doesn't produce a psychic cord between the two of you when you are asking God, the Life Source or the Universe to help while remaining removed from the process.

At the end of the session, as Lillian was leaving, I walked outside to the lemon tree in the back garden and picked a couple of fresh, ripe lemons. When I gave them to her, she immediately pressed one to her nose to breathe in the clean, citrus scent. When she sighed and smiled, it confirmed to me that the light was reaching her again. I was hopeful that over the next few months, Lillian would be able to receive nourishment from the positive people and circumstances in her life to sustain herself during her temporary bleakness.

METHOD 4: THE HIGHER-SELF APPROACH

A fourth way of retrieving information involves asking your higher self. This is the facet of each person that is already spiritually evolved. This eternal being understands what you have been through to have arrived where you are and what you are spiritually evolving into. Usually, meditation is the best way to contact the higher self and the effort is worthwhile for those who persist. It's possible to look ahead and glimpse yourself perfected and know what you're aiming for. Essentially, your higher self is the part of you that has read the book of your life to the end. It understands your innate talents, personal strengths and the areas that need further development.

I use this method for my higher-self readings and developed a process to reduce stress when reading for clients. For these sessions, I meditate for 20 to 30 minutes before the person arrives for their appointment. During the meditation, I contact the client's higher self. This person has previously sent me a head and shoulders photograph so that I know I have the correct person in meditation.

I then ask two questions the individual has sent to me before the reading. I can spend five to ten minutes asking their higher self for more details about these questions without the stress of knowing that the client is sitting in front of me, eagerly waiting for news but hearing nothing while I strengthen connections.

I use a digital recorder to document my answers to the questions before the client arrives. As I end the meditation, I ask the client's higher self to accompany me throughout the session to answer more of their queries. When the client arrives, we proceed with the reading, where I consult with their higher self throughout the process. When the sitting concludes, I say goodbye to both the client and their higher self. At the end of the day, I cleanse with a salt bath and a meditation, to ensure no trace cords remain.

This is a more complicated process. Yet, who is better to advise a person about life direction than the spiritually evolved part of that person who already knows that individual's future?

Similar to the higher-self method, some people who follow

spiritual mentors find it helpful to meditate and ask their mentors specific questions. Contacting ascended (deceased) masters can also be effective, although very deep meditations are required to ensure that the process is genuine and not imagined.

People who follow a living spiritual master can find it easier to contact them through meditation than to reach an ascended master. Although everyone already has psychic cords to spiritual guides, the process can be more difficult when people don't know how a guide might look or sound when they appear.

For lasting clarity when contacting spirit guides, your higher self, living or ascended masters, write down everything you see or hear in meditation for later reference. If nothing is recorded, most of what is seen or heard is likely to be soon forgotten. Sometimes incidental details can become valuable information when circumstances glimpsed in meditation eventually arrive and decisions need to be made. A name, face or room seen in meditation can provide a reminder when predictions occur.

Before meditation, ensure that you remove any distractions from the room, including phones, alarms, electronic tablets, children and pets. It can be difficult to return to a peaceful meditative state after being disturbed by sudden noises or movements in the environment.

Meditation to Meet Your Higher Self

1. Make yourself comfortable.
2. Close your eyes and take three deep breaths, releasing each breath slowly.
3. Mentally state, "I am safe. I will stay safe."
4. In your mind, count slowly from five down to zero, taking a few slow breaths between each number.
5. While counting down to zero, be aware of your surroundings and let these thoughts go.
6. Notice each new sound and release it.
7. Be aware of each sensation within your physical body and let it go. Notice it and mentally state, "I release this now."
8. Give your mind a chance to settle. Simply focus on a mental

image of each number as you count from five to zero.

9. At the count of zero, allow your whole body to relax. Allow your mind to become settled and still.
10. In your mind, imagine a staircase consisting of 14 steps leading down to a closed door.
11. Begin to descend this staircase, allowing yourself to drift deeper within with each and every step.
12. When you reach the closed door, gently open it. This door opens onto a beautiful, sprawling garden with ancient trees, vibrant flowers, manicured lawns and assorted plants. It's a garden filled with life.
13. Slowly walk out into this garden, following the path from the door, into the garden. With every step you take, remind yourself that you're drifting deeper and deeper within as the images in your mind's eye become clearer and sharper to you.
14. Around the next bend is a lush, emerald-green lawn with a bench seat beneath a shady tree.
15. Cross the lawn and take a moment to sit on the bench seat. Enjoy the cool breeze, the warm sun and the cheerful sounds of birds nearby.
16. In a moment, your higher self is going to approach and sit beside you on this bench. They are arriving now.
17. As your spiritually evolved self arrives, notice this refined part of you. Feel the strength, confidence, patience and calm that this part of you exudes.
18. In a moment, your higher self will give you some personal information. Listen carefully as they speak so that you can recall what was said later.
19. After your higher self finishes, you can ask one specific question that will be answered clearly. Your spiritual self will begin speaking now.
20. Thank your spiritually evolved self for visiting to share this information and watch as they leave you now.
21. It's time to retrace your steps to the path and then to the open door to conclude this process. Do this now.

22. As you stand inside the door at the foot of the staircase, release this scene. In a moment, you'll count in your mind from one to three and open your eyes, returning your awareness to the room and to your daily life.
23. "One" — take a deep breath now and feel the vibrancy returning to your arms and your legs. Enjoy this fresh, clean energy.
24. "Two" — inhale deeply as you feel the natural muscle tone returning to your whole body.
25. "Three" — take a final inward breath as you come right back to the surface. Open your eyes, feeling wide awake, refreshed, relaxed and revitalised, looking forward to the rest of the day.

This meditation is available on the Free Downloads page at **www.paulfentonsmith.com**.

12.
INTENSE INTUITIVE EXPERIENCES

Developing intuition provides a range of emotionally powerful experiences for spiritual explorers prepared to brave deeper waters. However, be careful before diving in, as the depths often contain strong currents. One of the most common mistakes inexperienced pilgrims make is being impatient. The desire to make significant strides with intuitive development in a single lifetime or a few years can test the endurance of the most determined spiritual seeker.

When studying with a friend in London many years ago, she endured day after day of no sleep, as her guides kept her awake all night for spiritual development. Six-hour meditations were not uncommon and her whole life was essentially put on hold while she trained with guides at night. The most direct path up the mountain is also the steepest. It's not for everyone. Choose your own pace.

There is a distinct risk to personal sanity in forfeiting sleep for even a few weeks. This is not a path I'd recommend. In a spiritual development group I attended in Sydney years ago, there was a sense of competition among some participants. In a single year, three out of ten people ended up in psychiatric wards, on serious medication and under the supervision of psychiatrists, because they were in a hurry. They lost touch with the physical world while obsessively pursuing spiritual realms.

However, most people prefer a more moderate path. It takes longer but can be shared with fellow travellers who support each other in the process. Even gentle pathways sometimes have intense spiritual breakthroughs. When these occur, they make riveting reading in a person's intuitive diary but can be both frightening and exhilarating. The possibilities are endless and include some of the following:

Conscious Astral Travel – While Sleeping at Night

This allows a person to astral travel at will, stop over with friends, explore foreign locations or visit the deceased. Learning to do this consciously requires patience, practice and determination but most people do it unconsciously while sleeping. While the physical body sleeps at night, the traveller body—a form composed of finer energy—slips out to explore. This delicate energy body doesn't need rest at night, preferring instead to travel without the restrictions of the physical form.

For some individuals, the traveller body simply sits on the bed while they sleep. For others, it departs for distant locations as soon as they drift off. Occasionally, the astral body of a friend is waiting to have a conversation or to travel together to a location or an event. (See Chapter 24 for more information on astral travel.)

Conscious Astral Travel with Friends

This involves group consensus, either while out travelling or consciously by negotiating with friends and agreeing to meet at a particular time. It sometimes occurs with the supervision of spirit guides or under the direction of spiritual mentors. This requires more planning if it's an arrangement with a living spiritual master in another country because of time zones.

Exploring Holiday Destinations Astrally

This is effectively like consulting an astral travel agency to intuitively glimpse a location before committing to a visit. Of course, the weather on the day of the astral stopover is not guaranteed on the days you physically visit that location. The sparkling sun and glistening sand on a Hawaiian island might be ravaged by a storm three days into your vacation.

Long Distance Astral Travel

These might include museums, towns, cities or specific locations. Using deep meditation, it's possible to visit foreign places to notice how different regions can influence attitudes and behaviour.

Meditations to Forgive Past Spiritual or Emotional Injuries

This can be done at any time and may become a routine for several weeks as a person resolves past spiritual or emotional injuries one by one. Although it can be an exhausting process, resulting in feeling tired the following morning, it often produces long-term benefits. These include freeing up personal energy for daily life that was used to endure old wounds and increased progress towards viable goals due to improved focus on present opportunities.

Programming Dreams to Explore Inherited Karma

Programming a dream is simple but take it one step at a time. Requesting a single night-time vision about all of your unresolved karma is a recipe for depression. Instead, ask to dream about one theme or issue that you can resolve or process now. Learn to walk before running. Resolving karma can trigger emotional and mental upheaval, so small steps are better than leaping into an abyss. It's not unusual to have sleepless nights for days or even weeks after a powerful astral experience about karma that is burdening you right now. Once you become familiar with the process, you can request dreams about more profound issues or unresolved karma.

The steps to programming a dream are simple. They need to be completed immediately before falling asleep at night. Make your request brief and succinct to avoid interrupting your drift into sleep.

Dream Programming

Most people roll on to one side just as they are falling asleep. At this point, say the following to yourself:

"Tonight, I'll dream about some unresolved karma and how I can resolve it. I'll remember the events of that experience all day tomorrow."

Relax and drift off to sleep.

If you sleep on your back or face down, simply wait until you can feel yourself beginning to drift off, then complete steps two and three. Keep a pen and pad or an electronic tablet handy to record your experience when you wake up or later the following day. Stating that you'll dream about how you can resolve the karma is essential so that you have a key to the next step.

Excursions to a City's Future

It's possible to travel into the future to explore the changing landscape of a town or city. This can be done in meditation. When in a deep meditative state, practise mentally moving forward one or two weeks to glimpse events ahead. With training, it requires no more effort to move ahead two or five years but be careful of proceeding too far forward or you might not recognise the city or even your home location.

Requesting to Meet Your Living Master

Your living spiritual master is the teacher currently on Earth who can guide and support your spiritual development in this lifetime. Through deep meditation, ask your higher self to arrange a meeting with your living spiritual master or mentor. Once contact has been established, it's possible find your way back to that individual for subsequent meetings in meditation. Simply thinking of that person when in meditation re-establishes connection.

Try not to ask trivial questions when meeting your spiritual mentor. Your personal development is the most important foundation. If unsure what to focus on, simply ask what you most need to know right now. Like any mentor-student relationship, it requires respect for boundaries and time to build trust.

Meeting Your Ascended Master

Your ascended master is a deceased spiritual master who oversees responsible for your development throughout many lifetimes. First, it's important to identify your ascended master. This can be done by reading publications from accepted masters or by asking your higher self or a living spiritual mentor.

When very experienced with meditation, it's possible to trace the psychic cord to your living spiritual mentor and then follow that thread beyond that person to your ascended master. When I did this in Greece in 1991, I had the assistance of a friend, Christine. It took several days of regular meditations and Christine lent me her guides to assist with the process. Without her help, I doubt that I'd have achieved my goal — to meet my masters.

Group Meditations

Group meditations with experienced people can provide powerful experiences and the opportunity to explore other locations, dimensions or alternative spiritual paths. Usually, the team practises regularly for several months or years, setting shared objectives when operating in a group process. Objectives can include venturing back in time to better understand ancient civilisations, exploring traditional symbology, or intuitive investigation of a particular location to compare notes on observations. However, once you're experienced, you might choose to avoid group sessions, as they may hold you back. This is especially so if there are too many beginners in the group.

Distant Group Meditations

In this type of group meditation, members are located across the globe. This involves meditation and astral travel, so it's for people more experienced with deep meditation. These groups usually have participants with wildly varying experiences, providing many different viewpoints of life. However, be mindful that they can also contain beginners or people who want to deliberately cord others to drain their energy.

Beginners are often not conscious of what their astral bodies are doing when away from their physical forms. The more conscious visitors who cord others are essentially energetic hitchhikers who want spiritual experiences without doing the groundwork first. To avoid this possibility, assess yourself soon after each session to ensure that you're centred and haven't taken on any additional psychic cords.

Exploring Paths Not Chosen

You can meditate with your higher self to explore a path you once chose not to take in life. This determines what opportunities a different path might have offered and the personal cost of not taking that direction. This process is rarely used but is effective if you cannot release thoughts about a job, location or a potential love relationship that was abandoned. It's also possible to ask what reward lies ahead for having chosen a current path. (See 'Meditation to Meet Your Higher Self' in Chapter 11).

Delving the Elemental Kingdom and Parallel Lives

It's important to remember that humans are not the only species on Earth and that there are parallel lives occurring between the physical structures that we take for granted. Just as there are constant radio and television signals surrounding us that are invisible to the naked eye, there are elementals existing in plants, rivers, oceans, clouds and beneath the soil. They are evolving in their own ways, unseen by us but often able to see us while we live our lives. It's possible to meditate to observe them. The natural place to begin is in your garden, a wooded area, a local piece of bushland, a river or a stream.

Examining Human Impact on the Planet

Through meditation, you can observe the past and present effects of people on the planet. This is not for the faint-hearted, as current changes to weather patterns and climate make it difficult to ignore the effects of humans on the planet. If you feel passionate about this, ask for guidance in meditation on what you can do to help restore balance.

Visiting a Sleepers' Class While Awake

Sleepers' classes are tutorials that some individuals attend when asleep at night but have no recollection of visiting when they arise the next morning. To do this while awake (in a meditative state) allows a person to see how these classes are run and to remember the details consciously. The traveller bodies of most people slip out of the physical form each night during sleep because although the physical body needs daily rest, the mental and spiritual bodies don't.

It's possible to request a memory of the night's travels when you wake up the next morning. This appeal is usually made just prior to falling asleep at night. It's best done when you can sleep in the following day, as you might be very tired upon awakening.

Glimpsing the Consequences of Your Actions

Through meditation, it's possible to see the consequences that your past actions and decisions have had on others. These meditations, when clear and accurate, can be eye-opening experiences. It's possible to understand why over-reactions occur and how unresolved issues subtly influence daily personal choices and behaviours.

Great emotional courage and commitment are required to undergo a 'consequences meditation' to discover the effects on another person caused by your decisions or actions. If manoeuvring to have a rival removed from your workplace ensures that you receive the next available promotion, that person might suffer from your actions. If this individual is then unable to gain another paid job for an extended period, their partner and family might also experience misery. The waves of this initial ripple spread outwards with consequences.

If this person is unable to secure a job at the same level due to age or qualifications, their children might not be able to gain higher education, resulting in less financial security for them and their families. The wave of repercussions from one selfish or destructive action can flow through generations. Although it is shocking to learn how personal desires have caused pain and hardship to others, knowing this can help an individual atone for what is essentially spiritual short-sightedness.

Being told in meditation that personal actions have changed your own life for the worse is difficult to absorb. For example, by pushing out a workplace rival, it's likely that you won't witness their promotion in that organisation. Had they been promoted, you may have become frustrated, to the point where you would have quit your job and pursued a new position in a different company. This other role you could have taken in reaction to being passed over for promotion might have led to more training and additional skills, resulting in greater personal success. By not glimpsing the bigger picture and forcing circumstances, sometimes ill-timed decisions make life more difficult for everyone involved. Your rival has gone, but so too, has a better job for you in a different company.

By redressing your personal selfish actions, it's unlikely to improve the lives of people affected by them but it is possible to minimise some of the karma resulting from them. In future, you're more likely to be aware of the possible consequences of your personal actions. Karma isn't punishment; it's basically an opportunity to experience what others have undergone as a consequence of your desires and actions. Karma allows people to decide if they want to continue on the same trajectory or to choose a better path.

Even modern businesses are gradually discovering that creating an environment where staff compete with each other for scarce resources, equipment and opportunities is a waste of time and money. While competitive workmates squabble and scheme, more cooperative companies often achieve higher goals because employees feel safe enough to work harmoniously together in teams. They're more likely to share ideas and voice concerns when projects veer off-course, because they know they will be heard and their opinions are valued.

Glimpsing Life's Bigger Picture

One of the most powerful rewards for contacting your higher self or spiritual guides is the opportunity to become aware of life's bigger picture. When immersed in daily demands, it's easy to forget your deeper purpose or even personal spiritual and emotional nourishment. By periodically stepping back from immediate anxieties to put life into perspective, it's easier to return to your daily home and workplace responsibilities with a clearer focus on personal progress.

Surveying the greater plan gives context to our personal goals, ideas and desires. When we're aware of a personal life theme or underlying lessons, embracing that experience removes some of the obstacles and smooths the path in life. With a deeper sense of purpose, it's easier to persist with small steps instead of becoming overwhelmed by unexpected complications. People usually have more patience with life's progress when they remember to shift focus from one day to a whole lifetime. Yes, actions taken in one day can shape an abundant life but they can also begin a chain of events that make life unravel.

During a recent reading, my client, Jacob, explained that he had spent more than 30 years studying a range of natural therapies and alternative practitioner skills, including naturopathy, kinesiology, meditation, NLP, flower essences, astrology, spiritual healing and hypnotherapy. Despite his education and several attempts to set up a private practice, he was unable to succeed. It wasn't that he was a poor business manager because, during this period, he had successfully built up a retail business that he profitably sold.

Jacob was tired from the effort and as retirement approached, he feared he would never be able to share his knowledge and skills with others in his business. Embarrassed to be consulting someone else instead of solving his own problems, he needed reassurance that everyone requires assistance from strangers occasionally. To soften his self-criticism, I asked him to assist me so that together, we might explore his options. He brightened at the thought of the two of us, with a pair of torches, carefully exploring a range of paths, options and possibilities.

Jacob wanted to know why he wasn't able to pursue his chosen career as a natural therapist. I suggested we divide his career question into six alternatives. He selected one card for each possibility. These were:

1. Private clients for natural therapy consultations
2. Teaching
3. Co-teaching with another person
4. Predictive methods (tarot reading, palmistry or clairvoyance)
5. Astrology
6. Other

The cards indicated a firm 'No' to alternatives one to five and a clear 'Yes' to number six, which was effectively another, different career. Jacob sighed deeply with a stony stare. He had the appearance of a man who felt that his only desire was slipping away from his grasp and even faster since the reading commenced.

I suggested that Jacob broaden the question to include a few different careers, again selecting six more cards, one for each of the following:

1. Natural therapies
2. Intuitive development
3. Predictions
4. Spiritual healing
5. Meditation training
6. Other (another—as yet unnamed—career)

Again, the cards suggested that none of the first five alternatives was suitable and that the sixth choice was worthwhile. He exhaled and muttered despairingly.

"In 25 minutes, you've eliminated every available choice I have. These are subjects I've studied for years. I've got a wall of certificates and diplomas at home and you're suggesting that I turn my back and walk away from the past three decades." He sounded angry and despondent at the prospect.

I asked Jacob his age and clairvoyantly ventured forward five years to see if I might glimpse him in a job or a career. I intuitively saw him working on a farm. The fields surrounding the glasshouse where he stood were packed with abundant crops. There were rows of tomatoes, zucchinis and peppers growing in tubs with a few sunflowers at one end. It seemed to be a testing ground for plants before he filled surrounding fields with them. His hands were grubby, the glasshouse was searingly hot and humid but he was a man who was happy in this environment, surrounded by living food.

He was working beside a couple who part-owned the farm with him and there were several seasonal workers. Upon closer scrutiny, I noticed that this small farm was a very tightly controlled experiment. They used no pesticides and were following Rudolph Steiner's guidelines for growing plants biodynamically.

Jacob was in charge of introducing new crops that he propagated in the glasshouse each day. The undulating slopes surrounding the homestead were a variety of colours, some shaded by the gradient of their slopes. He then spent a few days meditating on particular plants to determine what they needed to flourish in the soil at that specific location. These meditations allowed him to ask for clarity from his higher self before scanning the topsoil to discover what nutrients were lacking for the crop he planned to sow and what might best grow in that particular location.

I adjusted my gaze forward another two years to see the business had built a solid reputation for providing tasty organic produce, which was being trucked across the state. I described it to him this way.

"It's the equivalent of writing a book. Your regular meditations will give you deep insight into the soil, the best crops to plant in particular fields according to the slope of the land and how to produce luscious fruits and vegetables without resorting to chemicals or pesticides. Your studies have led you to this farm and your purpose is to design the exact plantings to suit the specific environment. You record your findings and teach others. What is discovered during these meditations is taught to students. You'll devise methods that will become a nationally recognised set of guidelines for organic farmers in the decades to follow. Like a book, your farming methods will be remembered long after you have gone."

"How will I find this place?" He leaned forward with intense interest.

"That's up to you. The past years you've spent studying are not wasted as you'll utilise your current skills in your new career. Perhaps a meditation to contact your higher self might be the place to begin." If he was going to be stilling his mind regularly, he might as well hone his strengths immediately.

Jacob seemed relieved at this possibility; his hope restored. He had no idea of the enormous effort he would have to make but wasn't deterred by hard work. In that moment, happiness seemed to be just over the next hill. He discarded the rest of his questions and began asking about this possibility.

"I have a friend in the country in a shared community with organic growers. Could Dave be a key person in all of this? Should I visit him and spend a week helping out to see what comes of it?" he asked, restless to get started on his life's work.

Sometimes people take the long way towards their purpose, gathering information and knowledge in the process. Jacob's journey was about to bring him to a location to combine many of his skills and talents in a rewarding career, growing food and feeding others. My mission that day was to encourage him to persist with his purpose while being open to unexpected opportunities when they arrived.

As he departed, Jacob vowed to visit every possible organic farm in the state to gauge if it might be a good option for relocation. He shook my hand vigorously and smiled with renewed enthusiasm for the possibilities ahead. I asked him to let me know when he found his new home. He was in such a hurry that he strode off, leaving his car keys on the floor beside the reading table. When he appeared at my window two minutes later, I quipped, "Back so soon? Found that farm already?"

13. PHYSICAL BODY INFORMATION

For people who struggle with meditation, there is a simple shortcut to intuitive information that's accessible to almost everyone. It's found through simply feeling and listening attentively to your physical body.

In psychic development courses, early on the first day, I usually request a volunteer and we complete a simple exercise. The volunteer stands still with their back to one wall in the room while I stand against the opposite wall. I begin taking slow, paced steps towards the person, asking that they tell me to stop as soon as there is any discomfort within the physical body. As soon as I am too close for comfort, I'm told to stop and I immediately halt.

I ask what part of the person's body experienced tension. I then enquire if that particular part is usually the barometer for stress in the person's surroundings. Then we reverse the process. The volunteer walks slowly towards me and I announce when I feel discomfort. This is training in how to pay close attention to your physical body.

In a recent course, Tanya volunteered and explained that she experienced a tightening in her chest as I approached. When she tried the exercise a few more times with different people, she discovered that same area of her body reacted as they slowly approached her.

To demonstrate the accuracy of body information, I asked Tanya to close her eyes and we repeated the exercise. I began from the other side of the room and she stopped me at the same distance as she had with her eyes open. I then asked her to walk towards me and to stop when her body experienced any discomfort. We repeated the process with her eyes closed and she stopped at the same point without any visual reference.

The body is constantly attempting to tell us about a wide range of experiences and reactions to people, conversations and circumstances. To understand it, it is necessary to pause, feel and listen thoroughly. This exercise is simple, immediate and free. For some students, its greatest appeal is that it's not meditation. It can be done with eyes open almost anywhere.

BODY AWARENESS EXERCISE

This process begins with the simple, internal question, "How do I feel in my body right now?" Then follow with other questions, including:

- What is my body currently telling me?
- Am I braced against these circumstances or accepting them?
- If I'm inwardly shielded from my current surroundings, why?
- What is it about this person, idea, conversation or experience that leaves me feeling this way?
- What does my body need to feel more relaxed, confident or calm?

For some people, the physical body is simply a vehicle for moving the mind to different locations throughout the day. These individuals often have limited awareness of physical sensations until they experience sudden pain. Agony is nature's way of shouting. To avoid physical distress, it's essential to pay attention when the body whispers. Then it's possible to notice discomfort, weariness, excitement and bliss. Otherwise, that tension accumulates, becoming more forceful when pressure mounts.

In contrast, kinaesthetic people are usually keenly aware of the full range of physical sensations. These individuals often need to touch others when conversing as a way to connect with people. I've noticed that if kinaesthetic people don't receive enough touching, they tend to eat more food. It's as though they receive their touching from the inside.

People who easily develop their awareness of the physical body can frequently make decisions based on hunches or gut feelings. They instinctively know when a situation presents an opportunity or a threat. Choices feel right or wrong to them and they are often aware of particular sensations in specific organs or areas that signify a 'Yes' or a 'No' when needing to choose an option. These are learned through trial and error with smaller choices and honed until they are a reliable source of guidance when major life decisions arrive.

Many techniques in this book advocate stilling the physical body and then ignoring it while focusing on the higher energy systems. Consider the information available if, instead, people simply paused and listened to their bodily sensations. Because our physical being is connected to each of our other energy bodies, it can link our mind to all available information, knowledge and accumulated understanding of those energy systems. When we take time to heed signs, useful feedback is instantly available. Pausing is the key. Some people find that meditation or yoga helps them to be mentally still, whereas for others, walking, jogging or repetitive exercise places them in the zone. Discovering what personally works best is essential for optimum results.

What might happen if someone stops momentarily to pay attention to the physical self while asking, "What is the next step for me?" In my book, *Intuition: Keys to Unlocking Your Inner Wisdom*, I mentioned that animal intuition is less developed than spiritual perception and that it is more often related to simple survival rather than spiritual direction. I've since discovered that this is not entirely accurate because with practice and persistence, it's possible to learn to ask the physical body what the next step is and instinctively know the answer. This process doesn't require meditation. It does, however, need focus. How different might life look if every time a decision was required, you had an effective method for making accurate choices?

For some intuitive development students who are more aware of physical sensations, gaining valuable information without meditating can be a relief. Listening to the body provides a simple, direct route to intuitive knowledge.

A friend, Max, finds vacant car parks by simply stating aloud that he wants a car park within three to five minutes and then letting his body tell him which way to go and when to turn. The first time I was a passenger in his car and he stated aloud, "I'm ready for a safe, legal car park and I'd like to find it within four minutes," I laughed and replied, "Yes, wouldn't we all? But you might need a missile launcher to create one."

Everywhere I looked, I saw cars cruising around in search of a spot. Max turned right into a narrow lane and found a sizeable park almost immediately. As we stepped out onto the street, he comically declared, "What a guy!"

"But can you use this skill to find us a vacant café table at Renaldo's?" I asked him. "You know, I've never tried," he replied, contemplating the possibilities.

Over coffee at our newfound table at Renaldo's, we discussed the potential of using instinctive intuition to find a new partner at a crowded gathering, a riveting novel in a bookstore or the perfect vacant but unadvertised office space for a new business venture. If a person's instincts can guide their hands on a steering wheel, it could point their feet in a crowded room or towards a specific bookshelf.

"I could use it to steer me with investing in shares," Max said excitedly.

"Steady on," I replied. "One step at a time and I mean that literally."

In the past, I've trained people who wanted to invest in local stocks, buying and selling based on intuition but this process is fraught with problems, not the least of which is desire. Yearning for free money or effortless wealth can overrule intuition, often with painful financial consequences. What begins as careful investing, based on research and due diligence, gradually becomes gambling, fuelled by the urge to recoup recent losses.

It's probably prudent to avoid using intuitive body sensations to find a new partner. Try telling a judge that you weren't stalking Mr or Ms Right but simply trusting your instincts when you followed that person down three streets and two dimly lit lanes at 2 am.

PUTTING PHYSICAL BODY INFORMATION TO USE

To begin working with physical body information, it's best to try one or two repetitive tests. These might include:

- Stating that you want to find a particular product in the supermarket and allowing your feet to take you to the aisle and the shelf where that product is stored.
- Declaring that you want to find a safe, comfortable, legal car park within five minutes and allow your hands to steer towards your objective.
- Affirming that you want to find where you have placed a lost item in your home or office and allowing your hands and feet to guide you towards it. This works only if that object is actually inside your home or office space.

BODY SIGNALS

Sally had been coming to me for private tuition in psychic development for a couple of months when she was unexpectedly retrenched from her job. She arrived for her lesson one afternoon confused about why she had not seen it coming.

"There was no warning. They took me aside at 4 pm on Thursday and I walked out for the last time at 4:30," she said. "Why didn't I have any idea that this was about to happen?"

"Describe what occurred within your body from 4 pm until 5 pm that day?" I asked her.

"I finished up a phone call with a woman in the design department and noticed my boss, Tom, and the human resources manager, Julia, standing near my desk. Tom asked me to join them in his office."

"What was your body doing?" I repeated.

"My heart rate quickened and I reassured myself that everything was okay."

"What did your hands feel like at this point?" I asked.

"I couldn't feel my arms and legs."

"Did your body temperature change?"

"Not that I was aware of."

"Did you find yourself soaked in perspiration later, after 5 pm?"

"Yes, I did."

"What were you aware of hearing as you walked with your boss and the human resources manager towards his office?"

"I felt a bit deaf now that I think about it. I suddenly couldn't hear the radio or voices, until he closed his office door and asked me to take a seat."

"And what was happening in the rest of your body while they spoke to you?"

"There was shock and the beginnings of panic. I had the strangest thought in my mind. I wondered what would happen if I couldn't stand up to go at the end of it?"

"You wondered what might happen if you couldn't stand up afterwards."

"Yes, while Tom was explaining that the company was restructuring the department and some people had to go."

"After you left the office, what did you do?"

"I went home and went to bed. I was shattered. I slept in my work clothes because I didn't have the energy or the motivation to change."

"Do you remember the 'walking towards each other' exercise that we did together in your first lesson eight weeks ago?"

"Vaguely."

"Can we do it again?"

"Sure."

We stood up at opposite sides of the room.

I began taking slow, small steps towards her, noticing within myself when I was entering each layer of her energy fields. Four steps into the process, she asked me to stop and I did.

"What part of you became uncomfortable?" I asked softly.

"I felt a pressure in my chest and throat."

"Anything else."

"No, that's it."

"Okay. Can I take one step backwards now?"

"Sure," she replied. I took a step back and asked her if this had made any difference in her body. She replied that it hadn't. I asked if I could take another backward step and she agreed. I did so and asked her again if it had made any difference to her physical body.

"Yes. I can breathe more easily now and the tightness in my throat has gone away too."

"If where I'm now standing is the point of discomfort, why didn't you stop me at this step when I was walking towards you?" I asked. She thought about this for a moment. I had actually felt myself crossing a line and entering another layer of her energy field at that point while I was walking towards her. It seemed that she had felt it too but hadn't told me to stop.

"I don't know," she replied.

"Is your chest and throat area where your body usually tells you that you're uncomfortable with your physical circumstances?" I asked.

"I don't know."

We ended the exercise and sat down at the table. I suggested that she cast her mind back to arriving at her office on Thursday morning.

"Do you remember how your chest and throat were feeling that morning as you arrived at work?" I asked.

"No, I can't remember. I haven't felt comfortable in the office for around two months now, as something has changed in the company. I don't know what but I had a strange impression that we were all on a ship without a captain or a navigator. I just remember feeling this sensation and panicking."

"What did you do when you panicked?"

"I went to the lunchroom and made a cup of tea. I then ate four chocolate biscuits and returned to my desk. Now that I think about it, I've been steadily eating more and more chocolate since that day."

"What did the panic feel like to you?"

"I couldn't breathe. I felt like I was drowning."

"Okay. Where in your body did you feel this?" I asked.

"My throat closed over and I couldn't get enough air into my lungs," she replied. Silence followed as she gradually made the connection.

"Could this have been your physical body's way of saying to you that something was wrong at work and that it was time to look for another job?" I asked.

She nodded, suddenly sad that she had ignored the earlier warnings. I sensed that she wouldn't ignore her body when applying for new positions in future. Instead, she would use her intuition to her advantage.

In the rush to have complex systems, tools and meditation methods to glimpse the future, it's easy to forget our basic, innate animal intuition. Although it's not as refined as spiritual intuition, signs and feelings in the physical body alert us to danger, change or opportunities ahead, if we pay attention. Then we can apply spiritual intuition techniques to clarify the best path to take.

A simple method for gradually becoming more aware of your physical body is the Quick Awareness Exercise. It takes two to ten minutes and can be done when walking, sitting in a car, reclining in a chair in a garden or just about anywhere.

QUICK AWARENESS EXERCISE

- Take a deep breath and release it slowly.
- Begin to state aloud or in your mind what you are aware of within yourself and immediately around you. You might say one of the following:

  I am aware of my breathing.
  I am aware of my posture.
  I am aware of the ticking clock on the wall nearby.
  I am aware of a bird chirping outside the window.
  I am aware of the warm breeze from the open window.
- Continue this process continuously for several minutes, speaking internally or aloud.

The purpose of this exercise is to become more centred. This means that you are increasingly focused, connected to yourself and to the ground or floor beneath you and not distracted by external demands. As you become more aware of your physical body and immediate surroundings, it's possible to feel more available to options in the moment. When distracted, it's easy to miss vital cues that herald positive change or confuse breaks for random events. One way to train yourself to become more aware of opportunities is to spend five to ten minutes at the end of each day reviewing events in search of missed prospects. Reflection can highlight possibilities missed during a busy day.

When someone is distracted by an unfinished argument, a recent loss or pressing hopes and desires for the future, that person is less aware of opportunities for happiness in the present. Escaping the present can become a learned habit, particularly for an individual with a depressing or frustrating childhood. This awareness exercise is simple, free and portable. It is a most effective way to release thoughts about the past or future and become present to the potential available in any specific moment.

I use this in courses to help students become centred before each day of learning. If they return from lunch energetically scattered, we repeat the exercise again to enable them to retain more of the course material in the afternoon sessions. Students can find it difficult to remember the subject being taught if they are not mentally and emotionally present when the material is delivered. Before we begin sessions, every person takes 90 to 120 seconds to tell us aloud what they are aware of.

As we work our way around the room, it's interesting to hear about what's visible from a range of different seating positions and perspectives. As we listen, we gradually become more centred, put a face to each name and voice and take a moment to hear from every student in the course. For shy students, these are sometimes the only times we hear from them.

KINAESTHETIC PEOPLE

Kinaesthetic (physically sensory) people naturally favour their bodily sensations when developing intuitive skills. Their bodies are reliable barometers when they learn how to interpret the signals. Naturally kinaesthetic people can easily develop the skill of reading the energies of environments, objects and people through touch. They sometimes experience difficulties translating what they feel into words for others. Occasionally, these tactile people also have well-developed auditory and chemosensory awareness. They are sensitive to scents and fragrances around them and are easily irritated by disharmonious sounds such as out-of-key instruments or shrill voices.

The chemosensory senses of smell and taste are associated with auditory awareness as the ears, nose and throat are clustered together around the throat chakra or energy centre. This means that a fragrance can evoke sharp memories of past experiences associated with a particular scent. However, sometimes a chemosensory person can unconsciously shut down their intuitive awareness and the five senses in reaction to a particular perfume or aftershave. Smells can trigger memories more rapidly and subtly than the other senses for some individuals. Therefore, it's easy to see how some people become completely distracted from the present moment by memories associated with past scents and sounds.

Energy healing, massage and bodywork, including osteopathy, physiotherapy and chiropractic treatments are often appealing to clients and practitioners who are tactile people. These individuals are naturally more bodily aware, noticing discomfort and disharmony through their physical structure more than through other stimuli, such as sounds or visual impressions.

The restriction for people who are essentially kinaesthetic is that they need to experience physical or emotional sensations to understand something. Sometimes, when dealing with a client who is experiencing conflicting feelings, this type of professional can become confused. If the client is afraid of receiving bad news, depressed about a recent loss or angry because they don't feel supported, the kinaesthetic practitioner may initially become overwhelmed by the conflicting emotions swirling around.

By developing auditory or visual intuitive skills, the intuitive reader can ask inwardly (auditorily) for guidance about which feeling to address first. It's also possible to examine the issues and emotions visually through clairvoyance. This provides some distance from overwhelming feelings. Clairvoyance (clear vision) can help highlight patterns, blind spots and entrenched habits before addressing immediate feelings.

COMBINING THREE INTUITIVE AVENUES

Successful intuitive practice usually relies on a combination of all three avenues (feelings, internal dialogue and images) to be most effective. Once a clear assessment of the client's circumstances is reached, the reader can approach the individual's issues through personal feelings, body sensations and what is being internally heard or clairvoyantly seen, both as patterns and as future opportunities. It's important to connect with a client uniquely, using the most effective process for each reading. It usually improves accuracy and insight, making the session more meaningful.

A kinaesthetic individual might respond better to a hug than encouraging words. Likewise, a sip of cool water on a hot day provides positive touch internally. An auditory person can find a calm, steady voice soothing. Conversely, nearby building construction might really annoy this individual. A visual person sometimes prefers an illustration (even with words) to illuminate important points.

When searching for a new home, take time to notice your initial gut feelings or body sensations upon entering the property. Some dwellings feel warm and inviting, whereas others carry the stale or hostile emotions of the occupants. In more subtle ways, it's possible to notice initial physical sensations when beginning a phone conversation or meeting a friend for lunch. First impressions can be surprisingly accurate but they're often buried beneath distractions of conversation or making yourself comfortable at a café table.

There are opportunities to practise intuitive development in small ways almost every day, when we look for them. From searching for a car park to hunting for a bargain, instincts can guide people towards their goals. With practice, intuition becomes a positive, supportive habit for life. It can steer an individual away from a stressful job, a poor choice of partner or an unfitting home. It can also alert people to positive alternatives and rewarding paths in life.

14.
DREAMING ANSWERS TO IMPORTANT QUESTIONS

When Karen came for a tarot reading, she asked about her lost passports. As a personal coach and trainer, she was more familiar with planning and advising others than asking for help. She explained that during one of her biannual clean-ups, she had carefully put the family passports away for safekeeping and couldn't remember where they were.

"It's a silly question really," she said with a nervous laugh. "I should have paid more attention when I was securing them."

"So, you've effectively hidden them from yourself?" I enquired cheekily.

"Exactly." I asked her to select one card while thinking of each of the following questions.

1. "Are our passports inside the house?" The answer was 'Yes'.
2. "Are the passports in my husband's home office?" No.
3. "Are the passports in the garage (attached to the house)?" No.
4. "Are the passports in our bedroom?" No.
5. "Are the passports in the spare room?" Yes.

As she left, Karen vowed to search the spare room for the passports and report back to me when she had found them. A month later she phoned to tell me that she still hadn't found them and was feeling rather desperate about her rapidly approaching trip. She was debating whether to cancel them immediately and apply for replacements before it was too late. She enquired if hypnosis might help to find them. Hypnosis can help people to access specific memories if used effectively.

I said that it could help if she had placed them somewhere. If someone else had moved them, then accessing her memory for the last movements of the passports wouldn't be useful. In passing, she mentioned that she had been reading my book *Intuition* and she liked the idea of setting a dream task to answer a question.

This process involves asking short, specific questions or setting a simple task while falling asleep at night. I suggested that Karen say the following sentence while drifting off to sleep that night. "Tonight, I'll dream about where I last put the passports, and tomorrow, I'll remember my dream." She did this and awoke before dawn the following morning, immedidate after dreaming about standing in front of a dressing table in the spare room. She fell asleep again and awoke later without an immediate recollection of her dream.

Instead of spending the day trying to recall her dream, Karen climbed out of bed and told herself that she would let her feet find the passports according to her dream last night. She walked out of the bedroom and into the spare room. She stopped directly in front of the dressing table she had dreamed about. Having already searched the drawers twice, she was sceptical but desperate. She immediately removed the drawers and emptied the contents again before sifting through them meticulously. She found her passports in less than 10 minutes. They had fallen out of a drawer into the base of the dressing table.

She emailed me excitedly to let me know she had found them and I playfully teased, "You've just saved money on a hypnosis session. What do you plan to spend it on instead?"

Although Karen's discovery wasn't immediately the result of remembering her dream, she recalled the full dream later that day. This is an effective technique for training your intuition but it does have limitations. Like all skills, it requires time and effort to build expertise. Being suddenly awoken by roadworks or a noisy neighbour trimming a hedge can banish all traces of a dream instantly. Sometimes, fragments of that dream might surface through the day but rarely the whole dream sequence. This is why it's important to write down dreams soon after waking, before life and daily demands intrude.

SETTING A DREAM TASK

- Set only one task per night.
- Personal instructions need to be short and clear. If the sentence is too long, it's likely to interrupt the process of falling asleep by stimulating too much mental activity.
- It is important to carefully consider the most effective way to set the task so that it doesn't take a week of attempts to eliminate alternatives. Instead of asking, "Is my purse in the car?" it's better to ask directly, "Where is my purse?"

There are many different methods used to locate missing objects. Setting dream tasks has the benefit of not requiring lengthy meditations or specific tools. You simply ask your intuition to work for you while you sleep.

If you don't want to sleep on each task or 'follow your feet' to find a misplaced item, asking for guidance during meditation can help, or simply cutting a tarot deck with a series of 'Yes/No' questions sometimes provide a speedy resolution.

FOLLOW-YOUR-OWN-FEET TECHNIQUE

1. Focus on a single purpose. This might be to locate your car keys, a friend in a crowd or a walking trail that leads home.
2. Ask your feet to guide you to where you want to go.
3. Start walking, allowing your feet to take you in their preferred direction. Remain aware of your surroundings at all times to ensure safety and to notice signposts or clues.
4. Stop when you have located what you need to find.

This process favours people who are kinaesthetic by nature. Individuals who can easily sense gut feelings or hunches are likely to enjoy early results with this technique. It can be done with other people too. In personal readings, it's sometimes used to intuitively follow the feet of clients into their homes or workplaces, providing information about these surroundings.

With experience, it's possible to follow another person's feet into a home from 10 years ago or a workplace five years into the future. Obviously, permission is needed when attempting this process to avoid trespassing into another person's privacy. There's more on this process in the next chapter.

For intuitively challenged individuals, it's probably best to avoid Alberto's technique. When he lost his gold band wedding ring, Alberto bought an identical ring as soon as possible to avoid conflict with his wife. Unfortunately, the second ring went missing two years later, so he furtively replaced this one too.

A few months afterwards, Alberto was unable to find the third ring and his wife Natalie noticed him searching for it. Being a natural observer, she sensed his stress but decided against asking him what was missing. Instead, even from a distance, she noticed him unconsciously fiddle with his wedding-ring finger repeatedly. Natalie decided to see if she could beat him to the ring and began her search in another room. In under an hour, Natalie had located all three rings around the house, her suspicion having activated her intuition. After finding Alberto's rings, she demanded an explanation. Her careful questioning revealed that Alberto removed his ring and watch when using the exercise equipment in their basement gym because they irritated him during vigorous workouts. Not revealing that he had lost the first ring cost Alberto an apology plus an expensive weekend away. "Buying another ring would have been cheaper," he sighed.

15. FOLLOWING FEET INTO THE FUTURE

In psychic development courses, we play a range of games to improve intuition and one of these is 'Follow the Feet'.

A volunteer stands before the class and we examine their feet or shoes. I explain that they are likely to wear these shoes home tonight and that we have an opportunity to mentally follow their feet home. It's a test to see if we can describe their home as they arrive there after the class concludes.

Students are encouraged to say what they see, feel or sense about the front door, the entrance hall, the living room and kitchen. If correct, the volunteer confirms the description. If incorrect, the volunteer says, "No" and we move on immediately. There is no shame or judgement about incorrect statements; it's only a game. The next person is then ready to say what they sense about the volunteer's living room.

I guide them through the process, beginning with the front door.

"They are opening her front door now. What colour is the door?"

"Look behind them. Does this front door open onto the outside, or are they standing in a hallway? Is this a house or an apartment?"

"Look at their feet as they step into their home. Notice the shoes they are wearing now, still on their feet. Expand your awareness to see the shoes and their surroundings. What can you see beneath their feet? Are they stepping onto tiles, carpet, floorboards, terrazzo, a rug, concrete or something else?"

Sometimes students become enthusiastic and even rowdy as the process starts to resemble an auction. When the volunteer has entered their kitchen, students are excitedly describing a wall oven, one, two and three-door refrigerators, single or twin sinks and a dishwasher in several colours.

They enjoy being able to speak without editing what they say, safe in the knowledge that they are allowed to be wrong. A few minutes into the process, one or two students have attuned themselves to the person's home and these individuals are usually more accurate from that point onwards. Once you have found that thread of information or link to the person, accurate information flows more smoothly.

We play this game each of the three Sundays of a course and students usually become more and more accurate. As they relax into the process, we're able to follow the volunteer's feet into previous homes, current and previous jobs and their next home.

Several years ago, a student, Bill, had been offered two suitable jobs and needed to make a decision the following day. Both positions offered good pay and conditions and he felt unable to choose the best option. We followed his feet into his next job four months from the current date and described the office. Bill immediately recognised it as one of the workplaces where he had been interviewed the previous week. It was a simple way to provide a glimpse of his most likely future without actually making the decision for him.

Bill phoned several months later to say that he had exercised his free will and chosen the other option. A month into his trial period, he realised that the job wasn't what had been promised and he resigned. He phoned the first company and was offered a position similar to the one he had applied for, as they hadn't yet filled that vacancy. Bill took the job and currently works in the open-plan workplace opposite the blue, mirror-windowed office tower that fellow students had described to him during the class.

When using this technique in class, students sometimes falter. When this happens, the volunteer is facing a silent group, some staring into space in search of a glimpse of the volunteer's home. I remind them to return to the feet and the shoes before them. Then it's important to imagine those shoes arriving home. When comfortable with the mental image, they are asked to expand their awareness to glimpse the shoes and their immediate surroundings. At any point, if they lose the vision of the shoes and their surroundings, they can return to the feet before them in the room.

Clairvoyants do this regularly during psychic readings. They'll mentally venture out, describing a scene that is likely to occur in the future. Once they have done this, they briefly return to the present before searching for another strand of information. It's about adjusting your gaze.

By following clients into their futures and describing various incidents or situations, it's important to provide some context wherever possible. People often have set ideas about what the future holds for them. By telling them about a different, unplanned outcome, some become anxious or depressed.

When Sabine sat down for a reading, she had the saddest expression I can remember seeing. Her eyes were a faded, pale blue and she seemed exhausted from constantly trying to please others while ignoring her own particular needs. She looked like someone who wanted to sleep for a few weeks and then wake up to better circumstances. I sensed that she needed hope that life would eventually be better than it had been.

During her reading, Sabine asked about her husband's health, his career and his happiness, so when I clairvoyantly glimpsed her living in the country and tending to her kitchen garden in her old age, she was confused.

"But Henry hates the country. He won't even go out of the city on weekends. He would never move to the country," she said with conviction. I hadn't mentioned Henry because he wasn't in the images I had seen. When I looked forward into her country circumstances, Sabine appeared to be single and happier than she had been in decades. I thought it best not to say anything at this point, as she already seemed fragile. Sometimes, it's more prudent to be considered inaccurate than to increase a client's current burdens.

In previous readings where I've described events that clients don't expect and don't actually want, they have left feeling despondent. One client who returned for a reading more than 10 years later said, "You never told me that it would be this good." I'm sure I would have told her that she would be happy in her unexpected situation but that often doesn't count when it's not a desired outcome.

The more background information available to the client, the easier it is for the individual to accept the changes required for the prediction to occur. In Sabine's reading, it was apparent that making her husband Henry happy was her primary purpose and her own fulfilment depended upon it. Giving her background details might have included describing a divorce, the sale of her home and more. Meanwhile, Henry had other agendas.

When Henry sat down for his reading, he stared at me coldly. Having a clairvoyant reading had been Sabine's idea and he dismissed the whole process as a waste of time. When I described a young woman who was not his wife, he acknowledged that he was obsessed with a secret affair that had recently ended. He had been in love with another woman for three years and invented regular "business trips" to ensure weekends together. Henry wasn't particularly interested in Sabine but remained in their marriage for convenience. When I followed his feet, I glimpsed a lonely man ending his days in a tiny apartment, wondering where his life had gone so wrong.

Instead of shocking Henry with details of his likely future, I traced back to see where it had all begun to unravel for him. The past created the present, just as the present creates the future. I described how his father had died suddenly when Henry was eight years old and he was expected to assume the role of the man of the house, taking care of his mother and his younger sister. He secured his first part-time job at 14 years of age and had worked steadily since. Adept at earning money to provide materially, Henry's emotional growth was stunted by the events of his early life.

As I described these events, his facial expression softened and when I acknowledged that he had an overactive sense of responsibility for others, to the detriment of his own emotional needs, he pressed his thumb and forefinger to his upper lip to stop himself from crying. He sighed, surreptitiously wiping tears from his eyes and quietly said, "I have to work. That's what men do." I agreed with him but explained that's not the only thing men do. I suggested that perhaps asking an eight-year-old boy who has just lost his father to "man up" and look after the family is too big a burden for a young child.

"Did this influence you to decide not to have any children of your own?" I asked him. He considered this for a moment, then nodded affirmatively. By searching for background information relevant to his current circumstances, I was able to see why Henry was emotionally unavailable and considered work and money to be the only worthwhile goals in life. To him, labour and income provided security and control over his existence.

During difficult readings, it is sometimes necessary to follow my own feet out of the room to gain some perspective. By stepping back from the reading table, I can better assess my reactions, motives and agendas. I can also ask my guides for the most suitable approach to difficult circumstances. Doing this helps me to give the best reading possible to help the client understand current circumstances more clearly.

Before attempting this, it's important to have clients' permission to intuitively explore their lives. Without consent, this is trespassing. Intuitive encroaching is spying, which is closely aligned with negative magic. Do so at your own peril. When people get into the habit of probing into the lives of others uninvited, they eventually come up against someone better skilled at the process and less interested in consequences of actions. This can result in drained energy, loss of sleep and health issues. In extreme situations, it can even derail a person's life. The following exercise explains how to intuitively follow someone's feet into their future.

FOLLOW-ANOTHER'S-FEET TECHNIQUE

1. Look closely at the person whose feet you'll be following. In the future, this individual might be wearing different shoes, so remember that you're following a person, not an outfit.
2. Glance away from the person to a neutral wall or a static view and go within, accessing memory and imagination. We do this naturally when we daydream or take a moment to recall a scene from the past.
3. Mentally follow that person into their home and gradually expand your awareness to include the surroundings. Begin to describe what you see to the client and encourage this individual to confirm what you see or tell you that they don't recognise the scene.
4. Give the person time to remember if this description fits a previous residence or a friend's home.
5. If accurate, continue to describe the person's surroundings before moving forward in time 12 months to repeat the process. If inaccurate, bring your awareness back to yourself in the room and repeat the process.
6. Ask the person's age. Now pick a time in the past (perhaps two years ago) and repeat the process. It pays to confirm accuracy by describing past events before giving predictions. If the client is uncertain, ask for their year of birth and then provide the year an event occurred and the age they were at the time it happened.
7. With experience, it's possible to move back year by year, or every three years, to infancy, confirming past events and major life decisions made through life so far.
8. Then move forward one or two years at a time, repeating the process of following the client into his or her life and then expanding your awareness to future surroundings. If you have a specific topic or question, such as health or career, each time you move forward, it's possible to look at that specific area of interest.
9. If it's a health concern, each time you move forward two or three years into the future, mentally scan the person's physical body

to assess their wellbeing. If it's a career question, simply move forward to a workday and expand your awareness of the person's workplace.

10. Encourage the person to provide feedback as you proceed because if you're describing their parents' residence, they might be staying with their parents for health reasons or after having sold their own home prior to moving interstate. If the home you describe is not your client's, intuitively check the property to see if they are sleeping there at that time. They might simply be visiting that day.

Please avoid diagnosing any medical issues and be sure to suggest that clients consult qualified medical advisers about any health symptoms you have described in a psychic reading. To the untrained eye, a range of symptoms can look like a specific illness but unless you are medically trained and have conducted the necessary tests, you're not qualified to speak with any confidence. Sometimes, even after routine tests have been conducted, experienced medical specialists can be stumped by a person's symptoms. These guidelines equally apply to legal or financial advice.

16. CONNECTING WITH YOUR INTERNAL GUIDANCE

Discovering what works personally in meditation, diet, spiritual and emotional nourishment, books or courses is important because efforts often bring benefits. Having a wise friend at your disposal who is gentle and kind and provides accurate guidance about avoiding some of life's potholes is priceless. It's also worthwhile if it helps reduce anxiety about the future and enables better life decisions, healthier friendships and more supportive relationship partners.

If using intuitive practices improved your decision-making by just 20 per cent, where might you be in two years? If you need motivation to use intuition daily, simply review your major personal decisions over the past 10 years and decide which of these might have been improved. Then ponder the possibilities that have dissipated as a consequence of poor choices. Opening a business that falters and is abandoned four years later might give you valuable personal experience but those 48 months are lost forever.

Through meditation, it's possible to contact your higher self and ask specific questions about your unique journey. The eternal self is the spiritually evolved dimension of all individuals. Because this part of you has already glimpsed the outcomes of many journeys commenced, your inner guide is well placed to advise or caution about currently unseen pitfalls or opportunities. (See Chapter 11 for more information on contacting your higher self.)

CONTACTING YOUR LIVING MASTER

When you are familiar with your higher self in meditation, ask how to locate and contact your living master. A living master is a spiritual master who is alive and well in the world. This individual might be a monk meditating every day in the Himalayas, a yoga teacher in a Western healing centre or a retired cleaner who spends most days learning, praying and helping others. The term 'master' is not gender specific, as it describes any spiritually advanced person who has mastery of skills and self.

Living masters are available to guide groups of individuals towards spiritual development, so it is important for people pursuing spiritual growth to seek out their unique living guides and connect with them. It's possible to visit a personal living sage in dreams at night without remembering any of the details in the waking state. Later, when you eventually meet that individual, there is usually a profound sense of recognition. It might be a first physical encounter, following many meetings in dreams or during meditation.

If most of this contact occurs during sleep at night, a person is likely to awaken each day feeling listless, especially when dealing with difficult personal development issues. Sometimes, it's not possible to meet a master outside of dreams due to time-zone differences, poor meditation skills or family demands.

While a living master is available to assist a person with their spiritual path during this lifetime, their main purpose is to remind the individual about a personal ascended master. This second master is a guide for souls after they leave this physical world at death. They can act as afterlife guides, escorting souls as far towards their final afterlife destination as their spiritual development allows.

It's possible for people who resist the guidance of masters, in this life or beyond, to assume total responsibility for their own spiritual development. However, it's likely to result in more measured spiritual progress, with learning and wisdom gained only from personal experience. Direct experience is often the slowest way to learn, as each lesson becomes indelibly, painstakingly imprinted in the heart, mind and soul.

BENEFITS OF CONTACTING THE HIGHER SELF

The process of contacting the higher self takes time and practice to fine-tune but when it becomes familiar, it is a powerful way to maintain a spiritual path. Eventually, with practice, it's possible to ask this spiritually evolved aspect about important decisions and their likely consequences. Heeding the wisdom of this inner part can help avoid pain and setbacks in life. It can also assist with maintaining beneficial spiritual practices for health and wellbeing.

When Rodney arrived for his first meditation lesson, he strode in, tossed his leather bag onto the floor and flung his keys in the same direction. He was passionate and impatient, both with himself and with everyone else. Not surprisingly, he was there because he wanted to improve his inner calm and experience deeper sleep at night. He spent many hours practising several different meditation techniques. These included observing his inward and outward breathing for 30 minutes, focusing on a lighted candle and walking at a measured, rhythmic pace while being grateful for the support life offered him. After months of meditation, Rodney was finally ready to request guidance.

The first few meetings surprised him. His higher self took time to guide Rodney away from some of his business plans, encouraged him to change his diet and explained that the world was his if he mastered self-discipline. Rodney considered himself to be focused and self-controlled, arguing with his higher self during these meditation sessions. Undeterred, his higher self set Rodney three tasks to be completed within three months.

The first was to improve his fitness by swimming in a local pool five times a week to siphon off his excess energy. When he was able to swim 15 laps of the pool without a break, this first goal would be achieved.

The second task involved being more patient with his wife and daughter. He could achieve this by reducing the number of times each week that he exploded or lectured them about their mistakes. When he admonished them less than twice each week for two weeks, this particular goal would be completed. This proved a challenging task, as he took a righteous approach. He lectured them and wondered why they weren't thankful for his valuable advice. Rodney began to observe their reactions to his volatile outbursts and was surprised. They either shut down or dismissed him and went about their routines as if he was simply a radio playing in the background.

His final task involved joining a meditation group that met weekly for spiritual development. Members read a selected spiritual book from the book club in between these meditations. Rodney had to participate in the book discussions without competing with other members or ridiculing people with different viewpoints from his own. At times it was excruciating, particularly when one member read a passage aloud, mispronouncing words throughout. He was scratching himself when he wasn't sitting on his hands, desperately resisting the urge to snatch the book and complete her task.

Basically, Rodney had to apply the newly acquired self-discipline he had learned in the pool while improving his physical stamina. He had to consciously become more tolerant and kinder towards his family while increasing his open-mindedness with strangers and their different beliefs. Rodney had not previously considered himself narrow-minded but he was keen to learn.

Twice during this three-month ordeal, Rodney was advised not to continually suppress all of his frustrations regarding family members and then vent noisily while considering this vociferous outburst one of his twice-weekly allowances. His higher self allowed Rodney to shout on the drive home from work instead. However, he was advised to no longer travel directly from work to visit a local gun range and fire off a few rounds for sanity purposes. Instead, he was directed to meditate before going to sleep after listening to the opinions of others at book club meetings.

It took him almost five months to complete his tasks, at which point he had chewed his fingernails down to stubs and wrecked two sets of mouthguards while he slept at night. It felt like years had passed when Rodney finally achieved his goals. As a result, his higher self offered more precise information about how to improve his intuition, when to hire another staff member for his business and how to be a positive support for his 15-year-old daughter Luci who was struggling at school. His higher self wasn't attempting to quell Rodney's passion but merely helping him to see how his furious outbursts created fear in his staff and family. These had cost him three valuable staff members in the previous year, as workers decided that the stress of waiting for him to explode didn't come with danger money.

Rodney learned how to channel his exuberant energy into more positive directions, strengthening his relationship with his wife and daughter in the process. In the years following this exercise, Rodney has thrived in his business and with family life. He has become an inspiration to his wife and daughter instead of being an unpredictable boss, parent and partner. When he feels anger building up within, he takes a long walk, leaving his phone behind so that he's not tempted to call someone and shout at them.

Below are basic steps for contacting your higher self. Take a few minutes after each meditation to write down what you have been told. There is a fine line between imagination and intuition, so there is a simple method for testing the accuracy of information supplied. At the end of each session, ask your higher self to tell you some specific details about what will happen in your life within the next 48 hours. Write this down carefully afterwards. Then two days later, check your notes. If what you've been told about the 48-hour period is accurate, it's okay to assume that the rest of the meditation was correct. If not, next time you meditate, ask your higher self how to improve personal focus, attention and precision.

The information given as a result of asking for an accuracy test is unlikely to be earth-shattering but it does need to be specific. "You'll receive a phone call from a friend" is not detailed enough for this test. If you're told this, immediately ask which friend. Resist the temptation to ask for the following day's lotto numbers to test precision. Your higher self is not there to grant wishes.

STEPS TO RECEIVING INTERNAL SPIRITUAL GUIDANCE

1. Set aside 15 to 20 minutes for a period of meditation. You might light a candle or play soft music if this helps. Simple, melodious music can screen out household noises or traffic sounds and a recording of white noise or waves can achieve the same result.
2. Close your eyes and take three deep breaths, releasing each breath slowly.
3. In your mind, become aware of any sounds around you, accept them and let them go.
4. Release the events of the day and allow yourself to be supported by the floor, a chair or a mattress beneath you.
5. Imagine a wide, interior staircase leading down to a door that opens onto a garden. Gradually descend this staircase, allowing yourself to drift deeper within yourself with each step you take.
6. When you reach the bottom step, open the door and walk out into a beautiful garden. A path extends from the door off into the distance. Follow the path and around the bend you'll find an area of lawn containing a wooden bench seat beneath a large tree. Cross the lawn and sit on this seat. Make yourself comfortable.
7. Your higher self slowly approaches from behind and sits next to you. Take a moment to notice your higher, more refined self. Listen as your visitor tells you one important observation about your current life.
8. Ask this sage a few questions, listening carefully to the responses. At the end, remember to request confirmation information about the next 48 hours in your life.
9. Thank your higher self and watch as they walk away. Know that you can contact that part of yourself directly at any time using this simple process.
10. Retrace your steps to the door and ascend the staircase. Count from one to three in your mind, taking a deep breath between each number while bringing your awareness back to the present moment and your physical surroundings. On the count of three, open your eyes.
11. Record what you've been told. Date your entry.

Once you are familiar with the process, you can request help towards meeting your living master. Consult this master through meditation or in person if they are close enough to visit.

Ask your living guide (in person or in meditation) about your ascended master. Seek information on your ascended master's teachings.

Be aware that sometimes people can feel overwhelmed in this meeting. They are often humbled by such presence and intense spiritual light. As a result, they can forget to ask any carefully prepared questions. This is fine because there will be plenty of opportunities to repeat the process.

It's usually a riveting spiritual diary entry when important questions are answered. Sometimes you're reminded to be patient about a process, or your personal persistence in the face of past obstacles is acknowledged. It's also rewarding when predicted opportunities arrive as you had intuitively glimpsed them, strengthening your confidence in the process.

Sometimes, deep meditations are powerful sources of inspiration that revitalise your inner strength or help resolve painful past experiences. They can also provide clear inspiration for song compositions, paintings or novels. More importantly, they'll eventually provide clear glimpses of the rewards of your current decisions and personal effort. It's easier to work hard when you're confident of eventual rewards for your labour. Intuition isn't always about helping others. More often, it involves improving your life by discovering how life circumstances and events have shaped you and how it's possible to reshape yourself going forward.

17. USING INTUITION TO IMPROVE LIFE CIRCUMSTANCES

Sometimes, despite many facts being available, a particular option ends in disaster. Imagine how much easier decisions become when you can look ahead to the possible outcomes of each alternative before making a commitment. Personal choices can be improved by using your natural intuition. This doesn't minimise the value of research, logic or taking advice from people who are knowledgeable. However, after you've carefully considered a range of options, intuition is a final tool to assist with positive conclusions.

Knowing when to change jobs, retrain to keep your skills current, or switch industries for a more rewarding career can make a huge difference to your income, job satisfaction and even personal health.

Shane is ambitious and focuses most of his attention on his career, using his intuition as well as taking the required practical steps. Surprisingly, he combines a can-do attitude with the discipline to meditate on outcomes and to trust his instincts when necessary. Restless and impatient, he is proactive in maintaining momentum to avoid boredom or losing a few years of his life in dead-end jobs. A former student of the 'life is short' school, Shane has no time for regrets. Instead, each setback only seems to make him more determined to pursue his goals.

With each mistake, he refines his skills and realises that simply requesting intuitive guidance when he feels stuck is insufficient. He's learned to scan his job, his company and his industry on a regular basis to be ahead of surging waves when there are looming changes. Anticipating disruptions allows him to prepare, reducing stress while increasing the chance that he can act swiftly when circumstances change.

Consequently, Shane applied for a new position at a start-up three months ahead of a merger between his current company and a competitor that resulted in mass retrenchments. The takeover was kept confidential, so none of the staff at his level knew anything about it. Although joining this young business was risky, his intuition suggested that within seven years, it would flourish and be bought out by a larger organisation. Part of his new package included company shares, which was a huge bonus five years later when he cashed them in and purchased an investment property to secure his retirement. Each of us has unique circumstances, so it's essential that we are vigilant for our own opportunities and pursue them in ways that suit us.

Everyone is born with intuition. Improving this natural gift is a gradual process, requiring regular commitment and vigilance. First, Shane needed to practise a range of intuitive techniques to understand which worked best for him. Knowing which questions to ask in meditation so that he didn't overlook anything significant was part of his learning curve. Some of these included, "Will I be happy with the outcome if I pursue this direction?" and "Is it wise to take this course of action?" Just because a person wants something doesn't mean that achieving it will be good or emotionally beneficial.

Having previously reached for goals that proved unsatisfactory, I've learned to ask with the proviso, "If this is right for me spiritually." Sometimes, what we believe will make us happy is merely a diversion from a more rewarding path. By including the stipulation that it is right for me spiritually, if I ask for something and it doesn't occur, I know that it wouldn't have helped me in the long term. This makes it easier to release those sought-after goals that, at first glance, appear to be butterflies but, with closer scrutiny, turn out to be moths.

Shane's intuitive process took several hours every week for more than 14 months. He said that it was better than hoping his company wouldn't be consumed by a competitor or that his new boss wouldn't be a workplace psychopath. Developing natural skills enabled him to avoid some setbacks that could have derailed a promising career. Time spent honing intuitive abilities can provide ongoing rewards, including decades of positive decisions with rewarding outcomes.

Shane's questions list below is rigorous. He didn't ask all the questions every week but covered all of them every three or four months.

SHANE'S CAREER QUESTIONS

- Are there any immediate career opportunities I need to be aware of now?
- Are there any immediate career threats for me to be aware of at the moment?
- What do I most need to focus on in my career at present?
- Is there anyone who can significantly assist me in my career plans in the coming month?
- Is there someone whom I can meaningfully assist in their career currently?
- Are there any courses I need to complete or meetups to attend to enhance my career in the near future?
- Is there a person that I need to be careful of in my career right now?
- What is the most effective approach for the successful completion of the current project I'm working on?
- What can I do now to ensure long-term career success?
- What do I best avoid to ensure lasting career fulfilment?
- Is there an individual in my workplace best avoided for smooth progress in the coming months?

USING INTUITION FOR FINANCIAL GAIN – A WARNING

After completing a psychic development course, 25-year-old Adrian booked some private lessons to train his intuition to focus on financial markets. He arrived late for his first lesson before explaining that his overwhelming desire was to make huge sums of money without leaving home. He planned to do this through a combination of day trading and other share-based investments. I tried to explain to him that using intuition to focus on strictly material concerns was unlikely to be beneficial but he was insistent.

"I'm going to be 30 in five years and I plan to retire at 30," he said, nodding with conviction. "I'm not going to be stuck in an office or half-asleep at the train station at 7 am every weekday. Besides, I can't live on what I'm earning now."

I paused for a moment, my mind racing while assessing his pitch. He would be granted an A for convincing himself of his plan but perhaps a D for its viability. I remembered being that young and part of me wanted to afford him a few more weeks of blissful delusion.

"Why should life offer you a free ride without any effort?" I asked him. Adrian waved his hands as he showered me with a carefully rehearsed range of justifications. These included how difficult his life had been and how fiscally responsible he would be when he was wealthy. This seemed like an admission that perhaps he hadn't been financially practical so far. When he paused after almost 10 minutes, I repeated the question. He was puzzled.

"Didn't I just explain my reasons?" he asked.

"Look. To be honest, I wouldn't even offer you a small, secured loan based on that spurious reasoning. What you've told me sounds like a man who cannot live within his means and who is asking for more money than he could easily spend. Why do you merit more money?"

"Are you suggesting that wealthy people are more deserving?" he asked immediately.

"Not at all. I'm asking why you feel that you are more worthy. I'm asking this question, and so far, I haven't heard a reasonable response." Adrian picked up his phone to scan through his list of reasons to determine if one could be argued more fully.

"Full marks to you for anticipating my question but none for answering it inadequately," I said. "Based on your reasoning, we are all worthy of incredible wealth. If suffering was the price extracted for wealth, people in war zones should all be millionaires."

He sighed, suddenly weary with the process. The light in his eyes faded. At that moment, I felt like an old man who was extinguishing his hope.

"Let's take the concept of suffering and turn it around," I said. "Instead of payment for past personal grief, what if a percentage of everything you earned through investing in financial markets was given to others to alleviate misery or hardship?"

"How do you mean? he asked.

"How about this possibility? While honing your intuition, maybe you could spend time investigating ways to give a percentage of profits to people who are struggling in life. You'd do it in a way that alleviates suffering or minimises hardship, and the more successful you are, the more ways you can explore to be charitable."

"You mean I send a payment each month to help others?"

"More than that. Don't simply send money so that you support 100 people working in a charitable organisation to meet their mortgage payments. Instead, you take the time to research someone who can benefit directly from your success. You might pay for an individual's education or help a child learn to speak English or play an instrument. You might pay for a cleaner to visit an elderly neighbour each week and clean her house or personally walk a dog of someone who cannot leave the house."

"Would it be a percentage of the investment or just the profits?"

"Just a percentage of the profits."

"What would be a suitable percentage?" he asked.

"What do you think would be suitable?" I asked. He thought about this for a few minutes, turning his phone over in his hands as he considered the question. Looking up, he studied my expression carefully to gauge my reaction as he spoke.

"Say ... 2 per cent? How about 3 per cent of all profits?" I sat quietly to allow him to hear his own words.

"If you invested $30,000 of your own money, would you consider a 3-per cent annual return on investment a profitable use of your money?"

"Hell no," he said instantly. "But they aren't doing anything for their 3 per cent."

"True. And you're toiling so hard for your 97 per cent of the profit." He shuffled uncomfortably in his chair. I guessed that he was struggling with suggesting 4 per cent or baulking at having to go all the way up to 5 per cent.

"What do you think is a fair share to give away?" he asked. I paused, remembering a teacher who once told me that charity doesn't count unless you feel the sacrifice after you have given something to others.

"Twenty-five per cent," I said. His jaw dropped at the suggestion. He sat speechless, too shocked to launch into his justifications immediately. I waited. I sensed that they were coming, so I took a deep breath and remained calm.

"That seems like a lot," he gasped at last. I nodded affirmatively.

"I hear you saying that it seems like a lot," I echoed.

"What about …?" he began and I cut him off immediately.

"Twenty-five per cent," I said.

"Why so much?" he asked.

"There's a reason for the percentage but I won't explain this just yet. If life is generous to you, the least you can do is to be unstinting in giving to others, don't you think?"

"But I'd be working hard for it."

"No, you wouldn't," I stated calmly. "Working 50 hours a week in a factory is difficult work. Selling newspapers on a street corner day and night in all weather is hardship. You'll be sitting quietly in an air-conditioned room at home, deciding how best to invest your money and where to park the profits."

Adrian looked at me and accepted that for the process to proceed, he would need to agree to donate 25 per cent of his profits to alleviate the suffering of others. Just as he resigned himself to the concept, I added one more condition.

"Given your background in banking, it's important that you donate anonymously without any tax benefits."

"Tax benefits?" he asked.

"Yes. We both know that donations to registered charities are tax deductible and it's not a donation of 25 per cent of your profit if it's deducted from your annual tax bill."

"But how ...?"

"Once a banker," I said.

Over the next 12 months, we met for regular private lessons. Adrian practised a variety of techniques at home until he was confident that he had honed a few effective skills. The most difficult challenge for Adrian was to remain detached from the outcome when he planned to invest thousands of dollars in a single trade. It was impossible to tell if his increasing success with day trading was due to improving his intuition or a result of daily meditation to still his mind and detach from his financial desires.

When he felt ready, Adrian ceased his lessons and continued his plan using his intuition and daily meditations. The carefully structured process worked well for him. It occurred to me that it wasn't necessarily something that everyone could learn because each individual has unique motivations, unconscious interference and different beliefs around money. Some people have negative experiences surrounding wealth that unconsciously prevent them from earning enough to live full lives. Others are more than capable of earning income but reckless in how it is spent. Some see money as a path to power, whereas others feel that wealth affords choices in life.

Almost two years after his final lesson, Adrian returned. His dishevelled appearance resembled a man who was surviving on energy drinks and take-away food. He looked nothing like the man I remembered.

"How is the process going for you?" I asked as he slumped into the chair. He explained that he had been losing money continuously for almost six months. At last count, he was down more than $60,000 and hadn't slept well since his losses began.

"What changed in the landscape?" I asked.

"Nothing. No … nothing," he replied, stifling a yawn. I tuned in clairvoyantly to see what had changed and it was immediately obvious.

"You stopped giving away 25 per cent of your profit. Did you become greedy?" I asked him directly.

"Yes, I had some big bills and couldn't afford to give so much."

"You can't now," I agreed calmly.

"These were urgent bills that I couldn't leave unpaid," he said defensively.

"At the peak of the process, how much profit were you making a month?" I asked him.

"Well, there was a peak period for about four months, and during that time, I made $15,000 to $20,000 profit per month."

"So, that's between $3,750 and $5,000 to donate per month. It must have hurt." He looked at me and I knew that he hadn't even worked out how much he had planned to donate. I nodded and asked, "So when did you stop paying the 25 per cent, or didn't you start?"

"No, I started."

"Let me guess. It was okay when it was small sums of money but when it ran into thousands, you baulked at giving it away." He nodded. It was time to further educate him.

"You made an agreement with the Universe but when you received good profits, you ignored your commitment. I'm glad I'm not your business partner. As soon as any shared plan was a commercial success, you'd be stealing the profits from under my nose. You thought that since no one was looking, you'd help yourself. What you forgot was that you didn't make the deal with me; you made it with Spirit. I was merely a witness. Those in Spirit are usually good at holding people to their agreements. You'll have plenty of time to ponder this when you get a job and earn a set income every month."

"I can't get a job. I've borrowed money to leverage my investments and it would take me years to earn it back if I got a job. You have to help me."

"I can't help you. I didn't do anything to take away what you were earning. You didn't make a commitment to me. What do you think the underlying lesson is here?"

"I don't know. I've been over this for weeks and I can't figure it out."

"I'll give you a hint. It's one of the seven deadly sins," I said and gave him a few minutes to remember what they are and decide which he had succumbed to. He reached for his phone and searched online for the seven deadly sins, then looked up and said, "Greed."

I nodded. "How do you expect those in Spirit to help you if they cannot trust you?" I asked softly. He wiped tears from his eyes as he put his phone away. The purpose for initially giving away 25 per cent was to develop the giving muscle. Forming a positive habit can meet resistance at first, but eventually, it becomes a viable part of daily life.

It's a perennial dilemma. When someone pursues a spiritual life, ethics become more important in how this individual earns an income, lives life and spends time. Finding a suitable balance between living in the physical world and pursuing psychic and spiritual development can be complicated. It often requires a reassessment of our old beliefs and attitudes and sometimes a review of friendships and relationships with others.

When someone begins daily yoga sessions or meditation, it's sometimes necessary to see less of a drinking buddy who is a distraction from their purpose. If a person takes up running or daily gym visits, it might be worthwhile giving up a weekly pizza night for more beneficial results.

"What should I do?" he asked. I felt compassion for his circumstances. Like Icarus, he had enthusiastically soared towards the sun, only to fall back to the earth, defeated. It probably wasn't due entirely to his charity commitment. Many home day traders make money on paper when they are ghost trading, then lose their investments when switching to actual trades. It can be a stressful process.

"If I was in your position, I'd begin by trawling back through my income since I began this project to add up exactly how much profit I had made. I'd then work out how much I agreed to pay to charity and what I had actually given to others. Then I'd pay out the difference … with interest. I wouldn't make big promises in meditation. I'd simply honour my original agreement."

Before the lesson concluded, we meditated together and Adrian left, humbled but with a renewed sense of purpose. He wasn't essentially selfish, simply someone whose fear of poverty fuelled his desire for more. I imagine his neighbours might be showered with gifts and support over the coming months. He'll probably enthusiastically help old ladies cross the road, even if they don't want to. Gradually, he'll come to know the feeling that accompanies generosity as he embraces life's abundance.

Because of the resistance Adrian felt to donating 25 per cent of his profits to others, I asked him to reduce this to 10 per cent. I then requested that he increase it by 1 per cent for every additional $100,000 of annual profit. He emailed a year later to tell me that he was making profits again and donating 10 per cent to support tutors for home-schooled children on the Autism spectrum. He explained that the raw gratitude from several parents overwhelmed him at times, especially when he knew that they were responsible for guiding and assisting their children 24 hours a day. He was discovering a different type of abundance — one that springs from helping others live better lives.

INTUITIVELY COMMUNICATING WITH ANIMALS

Dolph wanted to improve his animal communication skills to prevent his dog from terrorising the neighbourhood children. It probably didn't help that his canine was a huge, black, long-haired German shepherd named Wolfgang, or Wolfie for short. He brought the animal to his second lesson. I couldn't see how anyone confronted with this alert, quietly intimidating beast could bring themselves to call him Wolfie, as Dolph did.

"I don't want to communicate with other animals, just Wolfie," he explained. The dog eyed me stoically as if to suggest, "That's Mr Wolfie to you." If he was human, I thought he would make a suitable loan manager. He had a stare that might make people immediately reassess their appearance, their manners and the amount they wanted to borrow.

I closed my eyes (partly to avoid Wolfie's intimidating stare) and tuned in to the dog to ask if he was comfortable with Dolph communicating with him. Wolfie seemed fine with this. I then asked why he barked at children so much. He explained that when he was younger, a boy who walked past the fence daily often teased him. He didn't mind as the fence separated them. One afternoon, the boy appeared at the fence and threw a rock at Wolfie. He was startled and reacted immediately by leaping over the fence and snarling at the child, who fled for his life. Since then, Wolfie had not felt completely safe in his own garden.

To confirm the accuracy of what I was receiving, without opening my eyes, I asked Dolph if Wolfie barked more at boys than girls.

"I don't know. There is a boys' high school not far from my house, so not too many girls walk up the street, I think."

I asked Wolfie what might help him to feel more secure and more settled in his front garden at home when children walked up and down the street. He replied that he wanted to see more of the neighbourhood, to see where the other dogs lived and establish a larger territory.

I asked Dolph if he had time to walk Wolfie regularly to get him out of the garden and into the community. Wolfie needed to become familiar with the concept of his own territory and shared space and exploring the neighbourhood might help with this.

I asked Wolfie if he had anything to add and he told me that his master was moody at times and that he is sometimes afraid of him, particularly when he uses the axe in the back garden.

"Do you have an axe at home?" I casually enquired.

"Yes, I do," he replied.

"Do you use it much?"

"Yes. I have a wood fire and I like to cut the wood. It's good for tension," he explained.

"I imagine that you give it a good swing to break open the wood?"

"It's not worth doing half the job," he nodded.

"I only ask because Wolfie tells me that he becomes nervous when you use the axe in the back garden. Can you put Wolfie around the front when you chop the wood?"

"Of course," he said, turning to address Wolfie. "How's a big dog like you afraid of an axe?" he said, patting him vigorously.

"Perhaps he was a puppy when he first saw the axe come down and it frightened him?" I suggested.

Over the following weeks, Dolph practised stilling his mind and asking Wolfie questions. In the final lesson, I asked Dolph to bring Wolfie again. Wolfie seemed slightly warmer towards me during the visit, more like a diffident headmaster.

I tuned in to Wolfie to explain to him that Dolph wanted to communicate with him and that the only way he could be instantly sure that he wasn't imagining the whole process was for Dolph to mentally ask Wolfie to sit or stand or lay down and for Wolfie to do what he had been mentally asked to do. Wolfie agreed to this and I asked Dolph to make a simple, single request of Wolfie.

Wolfie stood up immediately and walked to the door, as if he was about to go for a walk. As Dolph's eyes were closed for this process, I relayed what Wolfie was doing. Wolfie then returned to his original position and sat down at Dolph's request. I was surprised when Wolfie walked over to where Dolph was seated and, before sitting down, placed his right paw onto Dolph's left knee. Dolph smiled and concluded the exercise, satisfied that he was finally communicating non-verbally with his dog.

I explained that communication is a two-way street and that each time he tunes in to Wolfie, Dolph has to ask if Wolfie has anything to say or any particular requests. Dolph explained that since he had begun the daily walks, Wolfie seemed more relaxed in the garden and barked less often at passing children.

"Two teenage girls even patted him as we walked past the park last week. Wolfie seemed okay with it," Dolph responded proudly.

OTHER WAYS OF COMMUNICATING THROUGH INTUITION

There are many reasons why people develop intuitive skills, from a desire to make better decisions to being able to communicate with a deceased parent or partner. For one determined mother, it was to be able to better connect with Ryan, her eight-year-old special-needs son, to improve his quality of life. Ryan exhibited delayed maturity and social reasoning, an unusually intense interest in freight trains and was sensitive to particular sounds, smells and tastes in food. These were some of the traits of his diagnosed Autism Spectrum Disorder.

Under the guidance of his psychologist, Kate patiently trained Ryan in the art of communication so that he was able to maintain more eye contact with people during conversations and recognise when he was becoming overwhelmed by people or surroundings. Sometimes, however, Ryan sank into long periods of introspection. During these times, he searched the internet for historical inventions related to trains, played alone in his room or sat in the garden on a wooden bench seat.

After Ryan went to bed each night, Kate often meditated to ask her higher self how she might better assist him to find his path in the world. Sometimes she would be given specific details on books to buy him (to broaden his knowledge base), slow exercise routines to teach him and methods to introduce new concepts, habits or positive behaviours. One night in meditation, it was suggested that she give him a specific book on George Westinghouse, a US inventor of the airbrake for trains. The following day she asked Ryan if he had ever heard about George Westinghouse and Ryan spent the next 40 minutes describing his inventions, how many patents he held at the end of his life and how he was an early pioneer of AC electric current. She later purchased the book, confident that her intuitive processes at night were accurate.

18. ACCURATE ANSWERS REQUIRE CAREFUL QUESTIONS

When Anna sat down, she asked the broadest question possible, "When will I be happy?" Wide-ranging questions rarely elicit precise answers, so I wasn't about to tell her that she would be happy at 10 am on the first Tuesday in November, four years from the reading date. It was a reasonable question. However, it was too broad for any tangible answers.

In a bid to narrow her focus, I suggested that happiness is a choice. I offered her a range of possible questions on the subject, including:

- When will I be in a positive long-term love relationship?
- Will I achieve my career objectives in the next two years?
- When will I be comfortable with my life?
- What can I do to improve my personal levels of happiness?
- Will a planned hobby, interest or new challenge increase my inner fulfilment?
- What can I change within myself to improve personal happiness?

An answer is only as precise as the question, so it's very important to give careful consideration to how to word queries when attempting to clarify important topics. Clear questions elicit specific answers or information and while it is necessary to ask open-ended questions at the start of an intuitive process, queries usually become more focused as the session proceeds. When Britta asked about her career prospects, she began with a specific query.

"Will I be offered the position I applied for yesterday?" When the answer was 'No', she asked a broader question.

"Will I secure a rewarding job within six weeks?" When the answer was negative again, she asked a different question.

"What can I do to prepare for the next step in my career?" She needed to undertake more study. I saw her completing two short courses. The first was a week-long course and the second was a two-day workshop. These two certificates increased her edge over other applicants for positions in her particular field.

A few months later, Britta returned for another reading, having completed both courses. She began with another closed question.

"Am I being considered for the position I applied for last week?" When the answer was 'No', she broadened her search slightly.

"Will I be offered a suitable job within three weeks?" The answer was 'Yes', allowing Britta to focus the rest of the session on other areas of her life.

When clients book a session and tell me that they only have one question, it's usually really one important issue they want to explore. Clarity often requires several questions. When Marianne asked if Claude would propose to her in the next year and was told that it was unlikely, she was naturally disappointed. Had she left the reading at that point, she might have been dissatisfied with the results. However, by asking what lay ahead for her in love relationships, personal happiness, family and career success, she was able to leave feeling confident about her future.

Sometimes people are obsessed with a former partner or someone else who is clearly not interested in them. When this occurs, I ask myself this question, "Why does my client believe that this individual is the only one who can provide personal happiness?" We all miss some opportunities in life because we are blind to them or distracted by life's demands. A clairvoyant sometimes needs to ask simple questions to clarify what the individual has missed and where this person became stuck in life.

Sometimes I ask inwardly, "What is the best way to deliver this information?" When someone tells me that I'm doing something wrong, I'm immediately resistant, tense and sometimes angry. If, instead, an individual suggests to me that there might be a simpler or more effective way to complete a task, I'm all ears.

WHAT DO I NEED TO KNOW RIGHT NOW?

Recently I was trialling a series of new questions that I might ask regarding clients who were receiving pure clairvoyance readings. These sessions use no physical tools or systems, such as tarot cards or hands to examine, or objects to hold to form links to clients. In these readings, I begin with only the client's first name and present age.

I need the person's current age so that I can differentiate between what has already occurred and what is yet to happen. It's easier to speak confidently about what has already occurred in the past but important to carefully construct sentences differently about the future because the client has free will to determine a final outcome. The future is fluid and there can be choices that lead towards or away from desired outcomes at any point.

Before my next client in the trial arrived, I meditated to centre myself and release any residual stress from the day. With the meditation completed, I had 10 minutes to spare, so I wrote out a few questions that I planned to ask my guides during Brian's reading process. These were:

- What decisions will progress Brian to his desired outcome?
- Will he pursue his intended path successfully?
- What would be useful for Brian to know about right now?

As I re-read the questions, I realised I had accidentally stumbled onto something unique and startling. One question of the three stood out from the others. I had asked a simple query that might turn out to be the most significant question I had asked in more than 30 years in practice. "Could it be that simple?" I wondered.

If all power lies in the present, what we do and what we ask in this moment has the power to shape all that follows. The question is:

What do I most need to know right now?

Clients often ask questions such as, "Should I move overseas to marry ___?" or, "Is it wise to take the job I've been offered by my former employer?" History tells me that many people do not do what is prudent. Some don't even do what they know to be smart, so this is only really half of the issue. The second part of a client's focus is covered in question two from the above list. "Will they pursue their intended path successfully?" is enquiring if the person will take a path to a goal and reach a desired objective.

Asking if clients will actually pursue a direction that they intend to follow is really the first question because if they won't, subsequent queries are redundant. If a particular client actively follows an intended path, it's time to ask question one: "What decisions will help this person achieve their desired goals?" By asking this question, it's possible to describe some of the major (and sometimes difficult) choices that will be required to reach the objective.

The most important inquiry is question three. If Brian is going to reach his desired goal (to pursue a financially stable creative career in video filming and production), he'll acquire new skills and knowledge in the process. If he was able to have some of the necessary concepts beforehand, it might make the journey smoother.

I have been so impressed with this question that I've begun asking it during my regular meditations each day. Becoming aware of what I most need to know right now is essentially a way of asking, "What am I unaware of that might slow my progress, derail my plans or distract me from what is important in my life?"

I don't want to end my life and look back with regret. It was wasted time if I end up saying, "If I had known then what I know now, the process might have been different." Hindsight is only useful if we have time left to change course. Hindsight, after the last breath is taken, is not really helpful.

If, after asking this question, I receive information that doesn't make sense to me, I ask for context or an example. As a clairvoyant, it's possible to give clients a few insights into what is useful to know right now but sometimes the ideas are not fully understood until they occur in real life. Learning is the process of internalising concepts and information through action and experience.

Doing is learning. If a person is likely to achieve a cherished objective—and in the process master additional skills and develop new self-awareness—they might hear a clairvoyant advise them what is useful to know right now without understanding when to apply this knowledge.

In a training workshop I attended decades ago, the instructor asked us to challenge the eagerly voiced opinions others expressed about us or our methods. She insisted that we ask ourselves if the other person's opinion was important to us and why, before accepting that individual's criticism or viewpoint. She then explained that it was possible to decide not to value another person's opinion and even to state this aloud if necessary. She suggested that this technique might be useful if a former relationship partner resurfaces to tell you what is wrong with you, your life or your attitudes. I thought about it for a while and let it go. Then, many years later, during a birthday dinner at a restaurant, I was seated next to someone I didn't know, who insisted on explaining to me why all psychics are frauds.

"How did you reach this conclusion?" I asked him, becoming impatient with his sharp tongue and blunt mind.

"Everybody knows this. Only an idiot would believe that stuff," he bellowed between gulps from his wine glass.

"So, no empirical research and no control group, then? No personal experience gathered from consulting a wide range of practitioners with recordings carefully scrutinised, cross-referenced and catalogued?"

"Let me just say this ..." he began.

I immediately interjected with, "It's a good thing that your opinion doesn't matter to me."

"What?" he asked with surprise.

"That's right. I don't care what you think. I'm here to celebrate

Cassie's birthday and you're just being a bore. I suggest that if you want me to take you seriously, go out and receive 40 or 50 psychic readings from a range of people and then we'll resume this discussion."

This was the end of our conversation and I was soon enjoying a lively interaction with someone across the table.

Having suddenly remembered that course I took in the 1980s and applied the knowledge that I have a choice about whose opinions I value, I discovered the power of this concept. By applying the theory, I avoided a night of resentment and frustration resulting from a conversation with someone I didn't know whose opinions I didn't care about.

A month later, I used it again during a radio interview when a member of a sceptics' association phoned in to ridicule me on air. After listening to his three-minute rant about charlatans and conmen, I said slowly and clearly, "You are entitled to your opinion, and I've heard it, but it has zero value to me. Enjoy the rest of your life. You can hang up now." He did exactly that and the rest of the interview proceeded smoothly.

WHEN ONE QUESTION IS NOT ENOUGH

Sometimes, a single question about an important topic does not clarify the options. As a reader, when a client seems confused or unsettled after I've answered a question, I suggest a few more queries on the same issue.

These can be open or closed questions. Open questions usually don't have 'Yes/No' answers, whereas closed questions are more precise. Both are useful but in different ways. If the issue is about current career direction, a person presently working in law might ask closed questions that include:

- Is it wise to study further in the current career direction?
- Would criminal law be a meaningful direction to pursue?
- Is it worthwhile my pursuing business taxation law?

- Will I become a partner in my current company within two years?
- Is it better for me to move to another company to achieve career success?

The same person might then ask some broad or open questions, such as these:

- Will I relocate interstate for a more rewarding career? (The client hasn't named a specified state. If the answer is 'Yes', they can then ask about a preferred state. This question would be a closed question).
- What does the future hold for me in my career?
- What is in store for me financially?
- What are my current career strengths?
- What significant opportunities are available to me in the next 24 months?

With practice, clairvoyants become experienced with forming questions for people. Sometimes a whole reading comprises questions centred on one important issue. Occasionally, a client wants to explore one urgent matter, despite having arrived with a long list of topics to cover in the allotted time. When this happens, it might be necessary for the person to return for a second reading later.

Here is a short list of simple, effective questions that can be asked every time you meditate or access personal intuition.

SIMPLE, POWERFUL QUESTIONS

What do I most need to know right now?

This question can provide insight into immediate struggles, obstacles and opportunities in that particular day or even in the moment. It's possible to discover that an important goal is likely to be abandoned in favour of another, more meaningful objective. Knowing this ahead of the events decreases a person's chance of becoming too overwhelmed to adapt to changes in direction when required.

What skills do I have that can be applied to my current goals?

This is a powerful question to ask when feeling stuck, powerless or ineffective. Schools, universities—and life generally—encourage us to be effective all-rounders but tremendous success often results when individuals play to their personal strengths. Find your forte and you've found what makes you unique.

What part am I playing in this current situation?

This is a valuable question to ask when circumstances are repeating themselves. This is the primary reason people develop personal intuition or consult clairvoyants — to receive an independent perspective on current life events. If a person is repeatedly struggling with an unrewarding life pattern, they have often exhausted all obvious avenues for change. An independent viewpoint can sometimes provide the insight required.

In my early days as a reader, I often referred clients to counsellors, healers, natural therapists and bodyworkers to help them change debilitating patterns of behaviour. When one counsellor phoned me to thank me for the referrals and to let me know that she had a two-year waiting time for new clients, I knew it was time for me to become a counsellor, to directly assist clients with their changes. Intuitive practitioners are only witnesses. Witnessing was not enough. I wanted to offer my clients more.

Is this issue something to be concerned about?

This can help anxious people recognise what is not worth the mental or emotional effort, so they can focus on more productive matters. If it is something to be concerned about, it's time to find an effective strategy to resolve the problem.

What is the underlying lesson for me in this situation?

Becoming aware of the hidden tests in struggles can sometimes help people to be grateful for the opportunity to master a skill or resolve a destructive behaviour pattern. Once the underlying lesson is identified, it can be learned, resulting in positive changes.

A clairvoyant is a witness — an observant individual who points the way when people are stuck or lost. Clients arrive enduring the burdensome consequences of past decisions and want to know if life will be different in the future.

The reader's brief is to illuminate some of the best choices the client can make to arrive at a desired destination. Another job is to issue warnings that are obvious from an outsider's perspective. Clairvoyants are essentially travel planners — for life's long journey.

Often a negative answer to an important question requires more queries to clarify a client's personal options. Don't simply ask one question, accept a 'No' answer and leave it at that. If during meditation you ask your higher self if you will be offered the dream job you've recently applied for and the answer is 'No', you will naturally feel dejected or frustrated. This is especially so if you've already applied for a range of positions without success. When this happens, it is important to be prepared.

Sure, you can sigh, swear or cry if it helps, but eventually, it will be necessary to ask a range of questions to clarify the career road ahead. Be prepared before asking the first question, to avoid several days or weeks of disappointment. These questions might include:

- What does the future hold for me in my career generally? (A broader question)
- Is it wise for me to pursue this type of position?

- Do I need to undertake further study or gain practical experience before proceeding with my career goals?
- Would this particular course propel my career forward?
- Is it time to change my career direction entirely?
- Would I benefit from interview-process coaching before my next job application?
- Do I need to hire a designer to improve my resumé?
- If I change company, will I be able to move up to a more rewarding job in the next two years?
- Are there better career opportunities in the present workplace if I stay?
- If I remain with the current organisation, will a suitable job opportunity outside the company appear within 12 months? (Is this bad timing for me right now?)

By clarifying personal options, it's easier to be more patient about opportunities that have not yet arrived. If additional study or new skills are required, the focus needs to be on these pursuits before applying for other positions. By asking some positive, careful questions, it's possible to move from waiting around for a new job to becoming someone companies want to poach from a current organisation.

Crystal-clear answers often require a range of questions. In the first week of January, I was trying to decide what book to focus on writing during the year ahead. I had commenced two novels and three non-fiction books but realised I'd make no progress spreading my time across five titles, so I consulted the tarot. I had a book in mind and simply wanted confirmation that this was the right project for the year.

I asked about each title, using a separate tarot layout for individual options and was disappointed to find that my preferred book would not progress well if pursued that year. The cards indicated that a different novel and a particular non-fiction book were best pursued, so I began mapping out how I'd accomplish these complex tasks. I usually begin with a large page and cover it in post-it notes containing ideas for chapters. Then I make up a basic timeline list on an A4 page and paste it on the wall beside my writing chair.

Reluctant to remove the existing page for the novel I wanted to write, I glanced at it repeatedly over the next few days. Then I noticed the page next to it on the wall. It was a timeline from the previous year that I hadn't managed to complete. It was a clear list for the non-fiction book. I had even written the current year at the top of the page.

"Look at this," I said to my wife excitedly, "I've made up a list for this title already. It's amazing."

"It's like … a prediction," she responded drily. "Ever considered turning pro with this stuff?"

If the cards had indicated that none of the five books in progress were right to pursue that year, I'd have asked:

- Is there another, more suitable book for me to write?
- Is there another more important project for me to concentrate on this year?
- Is my focus better spent producing videos this year?
- Is it wise for me to pursue writing a screenplay this year?
- Is it worthwhile working in partnership with someone on a creative project in the next 12 months?
- Will it be beneficial for me to focus on securing foreign-language translations for my existing titles instead?

Improved results using intuition are often the consequence of more refined questions, so it's time to begin forming queries around topics of interest and writing them down. Eventually, it's possible to have a template list that can be applied to a wide range of issues and goals.

Other enquiries likely to bring disappointment are emotionally loaded or long-range ones, such as:

- Will my partner and I be together for the rest of our lives?
- Will my partner die before me?
- Will I achieve all of my goals during my lifetime?
- Will I achieve spiritual enlightenment in this lifetime?

I've seen people who were happily married and then contentedly divorced two years later. Circumstances change. Often the desires we have in our 20s are no longer relevant in our 40s or 50s.

Sometimes, not achieving a desired goal can make way for an unexpected alternative. This brings a final possible question if all else fails. "Is there a better, more suitable opportunity ahead for me?" Then, a few weeks later, when you're exhausted from searching for it, ask, "How will I find this opening?"

The best, most effective meditations happen when our racing thoughts are silenced. A still mind is open to receiving large amounts of information in a single 15-minute meditation. These can often result in another 15 minutes of writing down what has been gleaned for future reference.

Just as one brilliant clairvoyant reading can provide important details for guidance through the years ahead, so too can deep, focused meditation. The benefit of meditation is that you don't have to wait 12 weeks for an appointment and be disappointed if your clairvoyant is having a bad day when you arrive. With meditation, you can simply try again tomorrow. If you're impatient, it's possible to take a brisk walk and then meditate again the same day. An additional benefit to regular meditation is that your thinking becomes clearer and your physical body is more rested.

19. "WHAT DO I MOST NEED TO KNOW RIGHT NOW?"

This simple enquiry is probably the most fundamental question a person can ask themselves. It can be posed every day with new results. It's deliberately open-ended enough to allow answers that might seem unrelated to current issues but can also be specific. Sometimes, when clients have exhausted their questions on an important issue and don't know where to go from there, I encourage them to ask, "What do I most need to know right now?" They are often surprised at the answers — responses that frequently require contemplation to fully grasp.

When Sarah asked about her second marriage, she was exhausted from trying to make it work. Before they married, David was a balanced, hard-working guy. Soon after the wedding, he began drinking heavily, lost his job and was working sporadically. Sarah then discovered that he was texting an old flame and attempting to rekindle their relationship.

She had already asked if it was worthwhile pursuing the marriage (it wasn't), if she could find a workable solution to their issues (unlikely) and if he would eventually settle into married life (a clear 'No'). When Sarah asked what she most needed to know right now, it was as though the microlens of the camera had suddenly been replaced with a macro, wide-angle lens, revealing her whole life with patterns of feeling responsible for everyone around her.

I intuitively saw her raising her younger sisters and an older brother while her father drank excessively and fought with her mother, who spent her days and nights gambling and flirting with men at the local club. As an eight-year-old, Sarah was already anxious while trying to be the responsible adult in the house. This became a life pattern where she took on co-workers' responsibilities when they became overwhelmed or were simply too lazy to complete their tasks. She even felt guilty about resenting their expectations of her.

Sarah had spent almost 40 years striving to move on from her bleak childhood to build a satisfactory life for herself but was constantly surrounded by people who relied on her for direction and support. These individuals were often too emotionally damaged to fulfil their own potential or too lethargic to master necessary skills.

"Who gave you this lifetime job?" I gently prodded before enquiring, "Can I see the job description, please?" and, "Did you apply for this role, or did you win it in a bad lottery?" I was attempting to help Sarah see that having clueless parents didn't mean that she had to look after everyone else she met for her whole life.

What Sarah most needed to know that day was that her childhood decisions had to be reassessed if she was to build the life she wanted and deserved. Sarah was disciplined, hard-working and solutions-focused but lacked a strategy for long-term goals. Everyone around her seemed to benefit more from her efforts than she did, including her uncooperative 30-year-old daughter, who was still living at home, rent free. Sarah was too busy working and striving day to day to think about who supported her or who took advantage.

"In your rowboat through life, who is in the vessel with you?" I asked. She listed a range of people.

"Who is rowing with you?" She silently considered the question.

"Who in your boat is actively drilling holes in the sides or the bottom of the vessel? Has anyone in your watercraft attempted to throw the oars overboard?"

I explained that anyone who obstructed her ability to earn an income, maintain good friendships, wellbeing or personal health was effectively throwing the oars over the side. Without oars, she is likely to drift endlessly on an open ocean. Someone actively sabotaging her efforts might need to be thrown overboard, either to retrieve the blades or swim to shore.

I reminded Sarah that by repeating her childhood struggle to compensate for incompetent parents, she was abandoning her profound life purpose. She had already been an actual parent and it was now time to pursue what she came into this world to do, before it was too late.

"Who helped you in life?" I asked.

"No one, really," Sarah sighed, suddenly deflated with my assessment of her life so far. I softened my approach, as she suddenly didn't seem to have the courage to fight off her overwhelming responsibilities. Sarah sat frozen in her chair, clutching her small, crumpled page of questions.

I looked ahead clairvoyantly to see Sarah becoming a late convert to assertiveness. Shortly, she was likely to move her daughter out to live with her father, divorce her alcoholic husband and invest wisely for a comfortable old age. I saw her travelling every year with an old friend who was kind, supportive and happy to row the boat with her. Sarah wasn't demanding huge rewards from life, as she eventually discovered the value of simple journeys to foreign places with a good friend.

LEAVING THE QUESTION OPEN-ENDED

Sometimes, asking, "What do I most need to know right now?" results in receiving guidance to make small, incremental changes.

When Jenny meditated and asked this question, she was reminded that she had recently abandoned her daily walks. Piers was advised that he needed to resume his morning tea break in the garden to soak up the sun. These simple habits provide emotional, mental or spiritual nourishment that helps build and maintain balanced, rewarding lives. When faced with pressure or overwhelming demands, people sometimes release positive, self-nurturing habits that provide vital nourishment. The results aren't always immediate but the effects can be lasting.

"What do I most need to know right now?" is a query anyone can ask daily. It's powerful because often what a person is most focused on in the moment is not necessarily essential knowledge at that particular point. When I've asked this question regularly over recent months, the answers have ranged from foods to avoid to chapters to include in books I'm writing and causes for current thinking and behaviour patterns. It's not enough to simply ask. It's important to listen intently, record the responses we receive and act on the answers to this question.

Resist the urge to narrow the focus of the question to specific issues such as:

- What do I most need to know about my current relationship?
- What do I most need to know about my health?
- What do I most need to know about my finances this year?
- What do I most need to know about my new workplace?
- What do I most need to know about my long-term career direction?
- What do I most need to know about my spiritual direction?

These are all valid questions but the original query is deliberately open-ended to allow unrestricted answers that can change our personal perceptions or even life direction. I'm glad I stumbled onto it. It has changed my life and the lives of clients I've encouraged to ask it as a daily exercise. It's pointless to focus entirely on a career of financial success when you need to address health issues that could derail your progress in a few years. An open-ended question allows the necessary information to surface.

When Janine received the same answer for 10 days in a row, she was extremely annoyed.

"I'd rather go for a long run than sit still and meditate," she bellowed.

"What have you heard for 10 days?" I enquired tentatively.

"To listen and receive. Listen to what? Receive what exactly? Pancakes?"

It was apparent that Janine was great at doing but less experienced with being still. I decided to run with the pancake analogy.

"Do you make pancakes?"

"Sometimes."

"Have you noticed that they require effort, coordination and then a rest before they are ready?"

"I just combine the ingredients, whip them up and pour them into a heated pan," she declared.

"And then?"

"I eat them."

"Yes. However, for several minutes between pouring them and eating them, there's a pause while they cook. There is effort and then a pause. Then more effort and a reward. The second activity is to remove them and put them on a plate and sit down to enjoy them. If you remove them from the pan too quickly, they don't have the right fluffy texture. If you leave them too long, they're burned. The waiting is every bit as important as the mixing and pouring." I paused to allow her to absorb this. She shuffled in her seat, fidgeting with her thumbnail.

"Would it be fair to say that in life, you're great at the mixing and pouring — the parts that require effort and action? However, the act of pausing for life—allowing it to prepare your next step—is frustrating?"

"Yes, I guess so."

Realising that Janine relished a good challenge, I posed the next suggestion as a question.

"How long would it take you to become as good with pausing as you are with planning and doing?" She now had a new goal. She was suddenly eager to master being still and patient.

Don't expect a particular answer when posing this question, "What do I most need to know right now?" Simply allow your intuition to find the most accurate and appropriate result that day. When a person anticipates a specific response, it can limit what is intuitively seen or heard. Sometimes, an individual is so close to a situation that they cannot be truly objective. That's a primary reason why people consult clairvoyants — to hear an outsider's view of current circumstances. If a psychic is a close friend or a work colleague, sometimes their objectivity is limited. If enquiring about personal issues in meditation, the quicker you can release your thoughts from the story you're telling yourself about life circumstances, the easier it is to be objective.

Try it out for yourself. If you spend five minutes each day asking, "What do I most need to know right now?" and listening within for the response, you will train your personal intuition and improve the results of your individual efforts. This process strengthens the links between the subconscious and the conscious mind. With practice, it's possible to ask this question when you're under duress and receive accurate, useful information to improve decisions at vital moments in life.

EXERCISE – WHAT DO I MOST NEED TO KNOW RIGHT NOW?

Quick version

Take a few minutes each day to ask yourself what you most need to know right now. Allow some time for an answer to percolate. Write down your result immediately for future reference and date it.

Deeper version

Meditate each day for 20 to 30 minutes, during which time you ask what you most need to know right now. Record your observations afterwards for later reference.

Thorough version

Meditate each day for 30 to 40 minutes. During this reflection, contact your higher self to ask what you most need to know right now. Record your results directly after each session.

RECORD YOUR PROGRESS

By recording personal progress, recurring themes and issues become glaringly obvious, especially when re-read after events unfold. Everyone has blind spots. It's difficult to be completely self-objective. In one meditation, I was told that a book I'd recently handed to a publisher would be delayed about a year but it would not be his fault. I was instructed to be patient and focus on writing my next book (this one). I sent the completed manuscript to him in 2019. In 2020, COVID-19 arrived, delaying the whole process. It was published in early 2021. Instead of feeling frustrated by delays and wasting time and energy trying to propel the book forward, I had anticipated obstructions (but didn't know what they entailed) and focused on writing other titles. This particular meditation saved me from months of frustration as the book's release date came and went without any real progress. Instead, it focused me on an opportunity that the pandemic lockdown provided — to write.

Reviewing an intuitive diary occasionally can also highlight underlying themes in career, finances, friendships or even sleeping patterns. Some clients tell me that they are too busy to keep a diary. This might be because their lives are too frenetic or that they lack strategy. They are too preoccupied to pause momentarily to make clear plans to achieve more with less effort. Lives without clear goals and plans are frequently unfulfilled by people drifting without purpose, who regularly take the paths of least resistance. Sometimes, skills we develop in pursuing smaller life goals are useful when embracing a deeper purpose. If someone is determined to climb Mt. Everest, it's probably safer to tackle a few less-demanding hikes first. Preparation is the key to achieving major objectives.

REMAINING ON YOUR INTENDED PATH

By regularly enquiring about what you most need to know right now, there is an opportunity to reconnect to those parts of you that have already seen your destiny and can provide clear guidance. If your future self advised of one small step to take each day to enjoy a more rewarding life, would this be worth 15 minutes daily? It might save you money on clairvoyant readings and, in addition, warn about bad first dates, underpaid jobs, micro-managing bosses, poor investments or buying a money-pit of a house. It could also steer you away from a great surgeon who is having a bad month, a job applicant wanting to embezzle from your business, or joining friends for drinks and needing a wheelchair after a car accident. We are all one decision away from a very different life experience and even small, positive choices can result in rewarding opportunities.

Sometimes people wander so far from their intended path in life that it's not possible to contact their higher self in meditation. Connections are intermittent or mediocre at best. At worst, they are imagined and inaccurate. On these occasions, it becomes necessary to consult more experienced people who can ask on their behalf. Gradually, with perseverance and practice, it's possible to develop personal intuitive skills to answer important life questions.

BEING OBJECTIVE WHEN READING FOR YOURSELF

I usually advise tarot students not to read for themselves because objectivity is difficult. However, many people ignore this advice. When they do, I suggest that "What do I most need to know right now?" is an important question they can ask the tarot or their personal intuition daily. At first, they don't understand many card meanings. Eventually, with hindsight, they develop a deeper personal understanding of the deck as well as their own life patterns. Some of these former students have learned to dispense with the tarot and ask themselves directly.

When I have a great idea for a book or a public talk, I take a few minutes to ask if this concept will be successful if pursued. I enquire because a book can take up to 1000 hours of writing, rewriting, researching, editing and revision without a guarantee of finding a market. This is wasted time and effort if I'm writing for a readership of one.

When the answer is 'No', as it often is, I'm deflated at first. What initially seemed crazy, original or life-changing suddenly appears pedestrian. Sometimes, I cannot let an idea go. Within a few hours, I've reshaped the concept and asked the question again.

Occasionally, I realise that I have saved myself months or years of wasted effort. If this doesn't brighten my day, I deliberately remember the hundreds of hours I spent designing and testing a board game in the 1990s that went precisely nowhere. I partnered with an artist who shaped the game board, the player tokens and the box while I worked on the text. We trialled it with around 120 people over six months, from friends to complete strangers. It also appeared in a 15-minute television segment when a producer heard about it and loved the concept but it was never mass produced. Eventually, I lost contact with the artist. Today, I don't even have the prototype edition of the game to remind me of my folly.

At that time, I could have written a successful book instead of creating a board game had I known to enquire about the outcome back then. These days, I ask a range of questions when I have a compelling idea.

- Will this idea make a successful book?
- Is it wise for me to begin this manuscript now?
- Is it best for me to partner with someone on this project?
- Would this make a better video, podcast subject or online product?
- Is this an idea that I can arrange for someone else to produce?
- Is it wise to outline this concept and put it aside to pursue later?
- Does this need to be refined before it is a worthwhile project to pursue?

By discovering what plans are going to be beneficial and which ones are likely to falter, it's possible to make better use of our available time. Sometimes, it's still worth pursuing a project that isn't likely to be successful, to meet people who will provide assistance with later ventures. If the answer to a project being successful is 'No', it's still worth asking if it is beneficial to pursue the plan and then enquire about the underlying lesson for completing it. Skills learned during one pursuit can be successfully employed in another, more rewarding endeavour.

Early in my career, I worked in the accounts department of a small company. Daily duties included chasing up payments for orders delivered to customers. Sometimes I wondered what I was doing there and so did my co-workers. Being young, restless and irresponsible, I found administration repetitive and tedious. I was a fish out of water. However, decades later, when I wrote a column for a monthly magazine, I needed those specific skills to ensure payment from the magazine publishers. Sometimes, when the editor dragged her feet with payment, I withheld my column copy until the funds appeared in my account. As this was long before electronic funds transfers, there were days when they sent an assistant out to the local bank to deposit cash into my account, especially when the print deadline passed.

I initially wondered if this process might be heavy-handed until I spoke to another columnist for the magazine at an event one evening. He hadn't actively pursued payments for his regular column and feature stories. At that point, the publisher owed him more than $10,000. He left the magazine soon after without receiving any payment. I was very grateful for previously having had a job that taught me the steps to making disorganised people pay for services supplied. That job taught me how to identify what was important (being paid for services) and focus on it. This particular skill has helped me to stay afloat in business for decades and I'm grateful for the opportunity to learn these techniques in an office setting.

20. FOCUSING A BUSY MIND

Intuitive discovery can be a startling process — especially when you've correctly predicted the outcome of an election, described the new home you'll be living in well before you visit the property, or intuitively glimpsed a friend's next relationship partner. It begins with simple hunches or body sensations that draw attention to threats and opportunities. With practice, it's possible to request dreams at night to answer life's deeper questions and to contact spirit guides for clarity or direction through meditation. Instead of making one more dubious choice that erodes years of your life, you can be guided towards more rewarding paths to your personal goals.

However, focused meditations that provide accurate guidance are sometimes hit or miss, especially if attempting them when excited, rushed or distracted by a busy mind. When COVID-19 arrived in Australia in March 2020 and our first lockdown approached, I meditated to find out when Sydney would return to some normality. I was told that I'd be back to work, with clients visiting my office again, towards the end of 2021. This allowed me to pace myself, knowing that we had about 20 months of restrictions.

When lockdown was briefly lifted in early 2021, I had a quick (distracted) meditation to ensure it was fine to take personal clients again. This time, I grabbed a few minutes between work demands instead of ensuring I had plenty of time to meditate deeply. Because I was uncentred during this process, I thought that we had escaped the worst of it and welcomed personal clients immediately. Soon we entered a period of more restrictions, including 107 days of lockdown. I eventually opened the doors to clients again in November of that year, as foretold in the more centred meditation of early 2020. It was a reminder that quick processes or shortcuts don't usually provide clear, accurate information.

Some people pursuing psychic development experience a few restless meditations and become frustrated with the process. A wandering mind or the sudden, shrill ring of a phone can interrupt a period of reflection. To prevent this, you might engage in light exercise for five minutes before meditating and remove noisy devices from the room to ensure a peaceful environment. When this seems impossible to achieve, it's tempting to give up, find an experienced local clairvoyant and be done with it. However, with practice, it's possible to eventually reach the next level of being centred and focused. This improves consistency and depth of information because the conscious mind is calm.

Sam found that writing down his main concerns in his diary before meditation allowed him to briefly forget his worries and focus on becoming still. He knew that they'd be waiting for him afterwards. Discover what works for you and use it. Anabelle consulted a clairvoyant to discover the best way to centre her mind for meditation, after accepting that she didn't have the patience to persist for months until she noticed what worked for her.

Accurate guidance is extremely difficult without inner stillness. A mind that is easily distracted has difficulty focusing on one important detail long enough to make sense of it. Briefly glimpsing information is easy but it's often without context, which is not always helpful. This can be clarified during a reading with a client by asking questions but when meditating for yourself, a quick glimpse can be confusing instead of illuminating. In meditation one day, I saw an image of myself decades ahead, having just viewed a film treatment of a novel I'd written. In this particular scene, I was despondent because the film director has not been faithful to my story. I felt disappointed with the final product.

In another meditation a few days later, I asked to see that scene again and enquired how I might find a more positive perspective. I was told to focus more on the large fee I had been paid for film rights plus the accompanying boost in book sales from people who would see the film. I concluded that readers who purchase the book would find the original story. Had I not returned to that scene in a more focused meditation, I might have felt stressed as the film was being made years into the future. Instead, I'll expect it and devote my time to investing the payment wisely.

Contemplation, prayer or yoga are also effective traditional methods employed to still the mind. For some individuals, meditation takes the form of repeatedly chanting a word or a sentence, while for others, it involves releasing all attachment to thoughts, feelings, ideas, urges and concepts. Physically or mentally restless people can prepare for mental stillness by walking, stretching or exercising briefly to improve focus. Any simple, repetitive behaviour allows the mind to settle, including jogging, swimming laps of a pool, knitting, walking, colouring an image with pencils or listening to soothing music.

When the mind is no longer attached to outcomes, concepts or ideas, it returns to stillness. Instead of resembling water in a gushing stream or a rapid river, it becomes like a lake, tranquil and calm. Still water in a lake accurately reflects the sky like a stationary mirror. If you try to identify objects rushing past in the brisk flow of a river, each item is only in view for a few moments. If, instead, you stand at the edge of a still lake, anything floating on the surface remains in place, making identification easier. The longer you can explore the scene of a mental image in meditation, the more information and context can be gleaned. Sometimes, focusing on a lighted candle for five to ten minutes is sufficient for the mind to become centred and relaxed.

These techniques (meditation, prayer, repetitive exercise or yoga), although different, can achieve the same goal: a calm, serene mind. Focusing on a sentence or a word is choosing not to be attached to other thoughts, feelings, ideas or worldly diversions. Conversely, noticing interruptions and releasing them as soon as they arrive in the mind reduces thinking and allows inner stillness to resume. This positive habit provides more consistently peaceful meditations despite sudden noises or loud conversations in other rooms.

An effective way to resist urgent distractions is to become aware of the part of you that is watching your mind. Pay attention to the observer, not the inner critic — who reminds you how you're not appropriately dressed for an event when you arrive or that you're sitting in a slumped manner but the silent watcher, noticing life. The part of you witnessing has a choice: to follow a train of thought or an idea, or simply let it go.

Be aware of the component within you that calmly observes other aspects struggling for control or wandering down dead ends that initially held so much promise. This perceptive part can dissuade you from thought patterns that activate your mind or trigger emotional responses that interrupt the mental stillness required for deep meditation.

When conducting guided meditations, I use surrounding sounds to deliberately direct students to drift deeper into a silent state of calm. If a train passes in the distance, I use this sound to steer each person towards a more profound state of meditation. I might say, "You can use any sounds around you to send you deeper. The hum of the train is helping you to drift … gently … down … within yourself."

Practise noticing every feeling and thought for a moment, releasing each one immediately. In a short time, this simple process can produce a sense of inner calm. It's also an antidote to restlessness by encouraging mental stillness. In this state of calm, it's possible to identify new options and make clear, decisive choices.

From a broader perspective, the soul becomes distracted from its spiritual purpose by an active or demanding mind. Sometimes it's necessary to quieten our thoughts to experience profound inner peace. In these moments, urgency evaporates, desires subside and tensions melt away. Time slows so that a 40-minute process feels like five minutes. Without the ordinary demands of everyday life or the yearning to be somewhere else, you can be totally focused in the moment. There, in stillness, it's possible to be at peace with the whole universe. At that time, there is no urgency, regret or desire. There is nowhere you'd rather be than where you are.

While mental distractions occur repeatedly, the mind is being dragged away from its focus by emotions felt in the body. These may be irritations about what someone around you has said or done, a desire to be heard and understood, anger at an injustice or grief at the loss of a friendship or relationship. From real emotional issues to perceived hurts, focusing on feelings during meditation distracts the mind from its true purpose, which is to make sense of life. Unaddressed emotions interrupt thinking and serenity, sometimes triggering restlessness. What begins as a plan to be still and reflect soon resembles a 3 am attempt to fall asleep while obsessing about work demands or the possible results of a recent CT scan. The more you think, the more there is to consider until the sun commences its ascent into the sky.

Emotions are also regularly diverted from their purpose into the physical body by desires: for food, survival, income, security, sensation, excitement or rest. At each level, individuals are constantly drawn down into lower, more basic levels of themselves, making it difficult to achieve the profound meditations necessary to clearly see life in context. Everything seems to pull personal awareness towards the physical world, so it's easy to see why many people struggle with meditation. The answer to this dilemma is simple but also sometimes elusive.

By gradually releasing every thought, emotion, desire and urge that distracts you from a deeper purpose, pursuing your personal life direction becomes effortless. It takes dedicated practice. Begin with 10 minutes a day and then move to 10 minutes twice a day for several weeks. Gradually build on this until it becomes a positive, unconscious habit. Try this simple process for two minutes and remember that it becomes more rewarding with practice.

Sometimes students cannot reach the 10-second mark without a dozen unwanted thoughts intruding. As they consciously attempt to control the process, the more frustrating it becomes. Imagine that you have just sat down in a quiet café. On the table is a menu. There is only one item listed on the faded card. It is one word: 'stillness'. Any time you feel distracted by intrusive thoughts or feelings, breathe in deeply and read the menu again and release the breath. Gradually, you can increase inner stillness from 10 seconds to 10 minutes. Thinking usually becomes clearer for several hours after this process. When this technique is used twice a day, complex choices seem more obvious and habitual worries are gradually reduced.

This short, repetitive exercise can improve meditations steadily. As a result, people often sleep better, feeling deeply refreshed upon awakening. Intuitive guidance received in meditation becomes increasingly accurate and focused. This can also increase your awareness of opportunities and your ability to make better choices.

We are the products of our decisions, so if you don't like where you are right now in life, try this simple technique. To motivate yourself, why not list three rewards you'd like to receive or experience from perceiving more openings in life and making better choices?

These might include a short-term goal within a year, a medium-term objective you'd enjoy within five years and a more distant goal in 10 years' time. Be aware that reaching these objectives might require study, acquiring new skills or improving physical fitness. If that's what's needed to move forward, these are small fees to pay.

EXERCISE FOR RELEASING DISTRACTIONS

1. Place a clock within eyesight or set a phone alarm to know when your time is up.
2. Make yourself comfortable for the next two minutes.
3. Take a deep breath and release it slowly.
4. As each thought enters your mind, instead of feeding it, let it go by mentally stating, "I release this thought now." If ideas crowd in, change it to "I release all thoughts now."
5. As each feeling surfaces, simply acknowledge it and let it go gracefully. As soon as you're consciously aware of an emotion, mentally state, "I release this emotion now."
6. As each feeling, desire or body sensation surfaces, acknowledge it and let it go.
7. At the end of two minutes, think back to how much of the process was taken up with releasing thoughts, emotions and body sensations crowding for attention and what portion of time was spent being still. This tranquillity increases with practice until

you look forward to each short exercise for the mental clarity that follows. A clear, focused mind can better direct you towards positive options and away from obstacles.

SEARCHING FOR DEEPER LIFE PURPOSE

With focus, all thoughts, visual, auditory and physical distractions that lead the mind in many different directions can be acknowledged and temporarily set aside. The energy expended in pursuit of those ideas and desires can be put to better use, which is to clarify your unique, deeper purpose in life.

Purpose is not the same as a life goal. Goals are what we want from life, whereas purpose is usually discovered in what we give back. You might want success, fame, a stable income, recognition or a sense of achievement; these are all worthy objectives. To explore possible underlying purposes for clients, I usually scan through their lives to identify what they have struggled with and conquered. People who have wrestled with specific ongoing issues and found effective ways to address these burdens are often well placed to teach or guide others who are restricted in the same way. A former alcoholic can identify with the challenges faced by someone trying to break free from alcohol addiction. Likewise, many counsellors and psychologists have had to confront their own personal issues along the path to helping others.

Having a profound sense of purpose in life with a realistic plan can increase resilience in the face of setbacks. The objectives don't change, only the path to achieving them does. Being aware of a greater personal purpose allows a broader viewpoint when obstacles appear. What might have once been frustrating or overwhelming is eventually seen as ripples in a pond, soon dispersed and forgotten.

Purpose is best when constantly acknowledged, making the mundane worthwhile. When I'm cleaning my office windows, I sometimes feel that this is a distraction from my work. By reminding myself that it's exercise to keep me healthy and it provides clients with a more enjoyable experience when they visit, I can see how small, incidental efforts contribute to the longer-term purpose. I have a home office with a long driveway that is beneath tall trees. I have to sweep up a constant stream of leaves which was initially very frustrating. Then one day, while sweeping, it occurred to me that this exercise grounded me by focusing me on the present moment. It also made me more effective in meditation and when intuitively reading for clients because it released body tension. I then applied that same realisation to every other aspect of my daily life that felt like it was distracting me from writing, teaching or meditation. Suddenly they all became part of my deeper purpose.

Someone who has failed with several creative ideas, due to a lack of persistence or poor planning, can identify their problems and become increasingly determined to prepare more thoroughly with their future plans. If a specific weakness is addressed and its opposite strength is developed, it might become part of a person's deeper purpose, to help others enjoy more fulfilling lives by expanding these skills or traits. If discipline or persistence are developed, a person has first-hand experience to motivate others to pursue these traits.

People with a sense of purpose often feel focused, confident and motivated to embrace life's challenges. They have deeper reasons to forge ahead despite setbacks because of their underlying determination to fulfil their personal destiny. No two lives are the same. Even individuals climbing the same mountain in life do it differently.

Discovering our life purpose is possible by remembering the past. By scanning your life so far and noticing the range of struggles and disappointments, it's easier to glimpse a pattern underlying these issues.

Juliette felt lonely. She made friends easily but everyone eventually disappointed her. When she explored this fundamental theme, she realised that it was based on her desire for excellence. In her mother's eyes, Juliette was perfect. As a child, this was a blessing, but in her teenage years, her mother's joy turned to harping criticisms of her perceived imperfections. While attempting to ensure her daughter remained flawless, she constantly made suggestions as to how Juliette might improve her actions, personal appearance and school grades. These disparaging comments no longer produced the desired results.

Instead, Juliette internalised her mother's disapproval, losing self-confidence and constantly fearing judgement from others.

As an adult, Juliette became judgemental of others, ending friendships and relationships when she noticed too many inadequacies. She accepted that the price she had paid for striving for perfection was loneliness.

Turning this habit around required effort and vigilance. Juliette had to begin by being less judgemental of herself. She was always well presented, with manicured nails, gleaming shoes and colour-coordinated outfits. I took a deep breath and requested that she practise being a slob around the house for one day each week and regard this as her homework. I suggested that she spill makeup on her jacket, miss one or two steps from her morning grooming process and leave some lipstick on her teacup. She winced at the suggestion but rose to the challenge. Being rigorously exacting and meticulous, it was exhausting for her to become the perfect slob for a whole day each week.

After several weeks, Juliette's next homework task was to be completely clumsy one day each week. Finally, it was time for her to eat a handful of parsley and take a selfie while smiling, with tiny flecks of green in between her teeth. One afternoon she explained how a woman at a nearby café table knocked over a teacup. The clatter of the cup against the saucer made them both jump. After initially frowning at the fellow diner's ineptness, it occurred to Juliette that it might actually be her weekly homework. She laughed at this concept and mentally admired her fellow diner for achieving her uncoordinated goal in public. By turning her desire for perfection into acceptance of herself and others, Juliette slowly and deliberately conquered an underlying theme in her life. As a consequence, she is now much more relaxed with herself and increasingly more tolerant of others.

When asked how identifying this issue and resolving it might be a part of her life purpose, Juliette wasn't sure at first. After careful consideration, she realised how it had helped her in her career. Part of her weekly job involved showing clients how to write and stick to personal financial budgets. She had previously struggled to teach people whom she felt were undeserving, lazy and self-indulgent. She assumed that their childhoods were similar to her own but this changed when she offered to drive a client home during a storm one evening. The elderly woman was overweight and unsteady on her walking cane. She felt overwhelmed at the thought of negotiating the subway in the rush hour, so Juliette insisted on delivering her to her door.

At first, the drive was tense, as Juliette's passenger Jeannie was covered in perspiration. This meant that Juliette barely took a breath in the first part of the journey while wondering where she could have the car professionally cleaned on the way home. Gradually, Juliette realised how far this old woman had to travel to keep the appointment and how she was always on time for sessions. Juliette began to think about how, despite the journey, the distance, Jeannie's knee issues and her fear of being judged, these lessons were important to her. She felt overwhelmed with compassion for Jeannie and decided to assist her into her home safely. Juliette was shocked at the threadbare carpets, the overwhelming stench of cigarette smoke and the putrid odour of cat urine as Jeannie proudly showed her around the tiny, crowded apartment. In that moment, Jeannie was no longer simply a client but a real person making the most of difficult circumstances.

After this incident, Juliette realised that some of her clients had never actually been shown by parents or teachers how to budget. They felt intense shame at being unable to manage their basic finances and as they felt less judged, regular clients increasingly became more open and honest about their failings. Gradually, with her acceptance of their circumstances, Juliette's clients became more determined to overcome their debts and rein in spending. They responded positively to her becoming an encouraging coach rather than a stern parent. Her ongoing success rate gradually soared as she assisted people without judgement and taught them new basic skills to reshape their lives.

Instead of feeling criticised, Juliette's clients became inspired because someone was aware of their struggles and attentive to their minute steps of progress each week. Gradually, Juliette learned not to apply a pre-formed budget to each person but to explore their individual circumstances and negotiate with them about what was possible. What had begun as weekly meetings with feckless clients became an opportunity to understand people and help turn their lives around. As a result, some of her clients became free from the burden of debt. Several could even afford further education to improve their career prospects and felt in charge of their lives for the first time. Juliette became aware of being part of a gift in someone's life and the joy of being able to help them with fundamental life skills.

As years passed, Juliette began to work with the children of her original clients, helping the next generation to control their spending and build wealth. She's currently writing a series of talks on the power of budgeting for school students to provide the basics before people find themselves drowning in debt. Her purpose has evolved in a practical way, helping people develop financial skills to navigate life successfully. Financial discipline has led many of Juliette's clients and students to enjoy a sense of freedom from debt bondage.

During pure clairvoyance readings, I sometimes intuitively move forward to glimpse the individual soon after his or her death. I mentally ask, "What did you come into that life to learn?" I listen carefully to the response. I follow this question with, "Did you learn what you came to discover?" Again, I await the reply before relaying these details to the client.

Challenging life themes can sound simplistic when we're unable to comprehend a person's history or emotional and spiritual baggage. Sometimes, painful experiences leave lasting inner scars.

During a recent pure clairvoyance reading, Anna seemed weary with life and undernourished. As she entered the room, she scanned me dispassionately and seemed disappointed that I was not what she expected. In younger years, that look of disappointment might have discouraged me, resulting in a stressful experience for both of us. Instead, I proceeded with the session as usual until, at one point, she shivered and said, "I feel goosebumps up and down my arms at what you've said. Those are the exact words my friend said to me a week before he died."

Intuitively, I sensed that Anna's life theme was about learning to trust. Mentally travelling forward to the final day of her life at 76, the older Anna mentioned how, towards the end of her days, she had pushed almost everyone away, trusting only her faithful dog, Oscar.

Then Sally, a nearby resident, found Oscar dazed and in pain in her own garden and provided a safe haven until she could alert Anna. Recovering from recent knee surgery, Sally limped up the street to post a note to Anna's front door, explaining where Oscar was. Several hours later, Anna arrived in a frantic state. It was a first meeting of neighbours and the beginning of a strong friendship when Anna accepted Sally's offer to drive Oscar to a local veterinary hospital for assessment. When Oscar was given the all-clear, they returned home before Sally hurried off to apologise to her cat for allowing a dog into the house.

As she aged, Anna struggled to trust her family and colleagues but she completed her life lesson through a sincere friendship with Sally, initially formed through a shared love of animals. Together, they volunteered at animal shelters and walked a busy neighbour's golden retriever puppy daily. During these walks, they were often stopped by locals who wanted to pat Oscar and the exuberant puppy. Soon, half the neighbourhood knew Anna and Sally by name, stopping them to share stories of their own pets. Sally was friendly and outgoing, a perfect conduit to the neighbourhood for Anna, who rarely socialised.

Anna felt that someone who was patient and compassionate with animals was a person she could rely on. Their bond gradually blossomed, healing some of the painful past experiences in Anna's earlier friendships while providing an opportunity to embrace her underlying lesson of learning to trust other people.

CATCHING NEGATIVE REPETITIVE THOUGHTS

Finding peace and stillness begins with consciously deciding not to waste energy on particular thoughts.

When Mia noticed that her boss spent more time talking and laughing with Suzanne, a nearby colleague, rather than Mia, she began to compare herself with Suzanne. Soon Mia was studying Suzanne's stylish clothing, resenting her bright, white teeth and her easy manner with people. In contrast, Mia was often clad in grey and black, as if to deliberately blend into her office surroundings. Mia shared an office with Suzanne but their lives were very different.

Instead of focusing on her own unique qualities, Mia began to wonder if she would become popular at work if she behaved more like her colleague. When she caught herself feeling ignored, angry or insignificant next to Suzanne, Mia knew that it was time to release her self-destructive assumptions and not waste any more energy. Thoughts need fuel to thrive. When we give too much attention or focus to specific beliefs or perceptions, it can stimulate compulsive thinking. Mia simply decided not to indulge her own insecurities and instead focused her attention more productively on her work and her own life. Every time Mia noticed herself feeling invisible, tired or nervous, she re-checked her beliefs. In the process, she discovered that adverse thoughts often accompanied negative feelings.

Many of these concepts were conjured in her mind. Mia imagined that Suzanne earned much more than she did, had a partner who showered her with gifts, trips overseas and weekends away and made friends effortlessly. She also told herself that Suzanne probably discarded her friends just as easily.

As this pattern of resentment became a habit, Mia consciously chose to regularly notice her comparative thinking and decided not to allow it to grow. At first, she was appalled at how often she was worrying about what others thought of her. In the first week, it averaged 40 times a day. By week three, Mia had reduced this to 14 times daily, as she made a game of catching herself allowing her worrying habits to dictate her thinking. Gradually, she noticed that she was beginning to feel more positive and centred as a result. She no longer left the office each day feeling exhausted or irritable as she once did. Instead, she had surplus energy for social activities and an ongoing cooking course.

This began a new challenge, where Mia became aware of as many of her own thoughts as possible in the course of a day, fortifying only those that bolstered her self-worth or deeper purpose. She also focused on wearing brighter colours to reduce the likelihood of being ignored by co-workers. Those negative thoughts—that initially required constant vigilance and concentration—eventually became a simple, constructive habit.

Because Mia felt more positive, she began chatting to work colleagues, who responded by including her in more of their social interactions. Once a week, she would bake a dessert and bring it to work, leaving it in the lunchroom with a note to her colleagues to help themselves. Soon there was a request to list the ingredients of each new dessert for people with allergies. Her cooking lessons were clearly a success, especially when she began baking vegan versions of her desserts each week.

Inspired by Mia's efforts, her fellow workers began bringing flowers and fruits from their gardens to share with colleagues. When one workmate arrived with a large bowl of freshly picked lemons, someone supplied a cheeky accompaniment of a miniature bottle of tequila and a saltshaker.

A few months later, Mia extended this self-awareness technique to include feelings and desires. Consequently, she managed to reduce her daily coffee and chocolate intake, shorten the time she felt bad after being ignored by her partner or her boss and more rapidly bounce back from emotional setbacks. Gradually, she noticed that she had more physical energy as a result of deliberately dismissing negative thinking or emotions.

Mia also discovered that as more of her attention became focused on her daily tasks, she required less effort to do her job. This allowed her to attend a range of meetups and an evening course and steadily widen her social circle, both outside and within her company. Over several months, Mia successfully changed some thinking habits and then several behaviours, improving her sense of connection with workmates and forming deeper friendships with some of them. More importantly, she changed how she perceived herself. Instead of struggling, she thrived.

MANY PATHS TO A STILL MIND

For physically agitated people, a walk or a brief period of exercise helps the mind to settle so that meditation can provide stillness. Exhausting the physical body is essential for people who are physically overactive or mentally restless. I find that mowing the lawn is sufficiently tiring to ensure a deep meditation. Recently, my wife was staring out the window at the overgrown grass before she calmly said, "You can't have had any deep meditations recently. Look how tall the lawn is out there."

Discover what works for you. A restful mind is still and neutral and allows deeper intuitive sensations to be acknowledged. When your mind is still, there is room to observe your surroundings, listen within and be creative. When a person feels centred, deep meditation can provide valuable information about their current circumstances, new opportunities or looming pitfalls. Sometimes, a good week simply involves avoiding making negative decisions that would result in a bad week.

Changing entrenched habits is rarely easy. It is often less enticing in a world where quick, simple or instant are usually desired options. There's no need to feel frustrated when comparing yourself with others who find meditation easy. Everyone is unique, with different skills and abilities. Discovering personal stillness, like any worthwhile goal, requires perseverance and focus. If you find it once, it's easier to return to it. It's the same with meditations filled with spiritual light. If you experience being in a state of grace or being filled with spiritual light once, you can experience it repeatedly. Like visiting a friend, the more you return to the person's address, the easier it is to find it again.

Each time you centre yourself or still your mind, you're strengthening the pathway to repeating this process with less effort. Establishing positive habits requires the same effort as forming bad habits. They simply provide different results. If your average week consists of a range of outdated or unrewarding habits, you can revisit the past to discover where they were introduced or simply choose to create more positive behaviours instead. Either way, you'll need to eventually form better habits, so you might as well begin today. Go on; challenge yourself to improve one single aspect of yourself, your thinking or your life. With each success, the next change seems easier. Eventually, you'll be eligible for the elusive *I wasn't always this fabulous* t-shirt.

21. EXAMINING THE PAST BEFORE PREDICTING THE FUTURE

Reflection on our past personal choices and their consequences can provide insights when making important decisions to disrupt our unrewarding habits. However, noticing life patterns requires time and freedom from distractions. Annual holidays, periods between jobs or while convalescing after illness, or times when we are away from daily demands provide opportunities to reflect. However, it's easy to examine approaching events and possibilities immediately, without leaving home, to glimpse the consequences of our decisions before making a choice. This can alleviate some of the stress experienced in selecting the best option and can be vital for people with a history of making poor decisions.

Developing our personal intuition provides a chance to look ahead at events before they occur. This can help with avoiding some of life's obstacles or assist with preparation for approaching milestones and opportunities. A lot of time and effort can be saved by looking further down the road. Exploring career options before being made redundant is a distinct advantage. This usually minimises stress and allows a smooth transition from one job to another. Intuitively scanning a potential future home for hidden issues can help avoid sudden, unexpected expenses.

When times are bleak, securing a glimpse of a glorious approaching summer provides confidence to forge ahead with plans. However, when sensing a dire future, it's time to explore alternatives. Often, looking ahead affords us time to carefully examine what decisions and actions need to be established to avoid unwelcome outcomes. Glancing ahead allows time to change course to avoid a searing disappointment. At the very least, after looking ahead, glancing back at our past choices can reveal the likely consequences of the directions chosen. Sometimes, scanning back further to childhood can highlight how our life perceptions were initially formed. Some people discover a family tree littered with poor choices.

A fatalistic person might simply accept this destiny, feeling powerless in the process. If someone wants a different outcome, the time to change direction is now. Sometimes, however, even with the best intentions, people fail to take the necessary steps to alter an outcome. Often this is because of the past. History shapes the present as much as current circumstances influence the future. If earlier decisions have incurred upheaval, stress or hardship, it's time to make different choices. This doesn't mean that every traumatic experience can be avoided but many can. Instead of putting out spot fires, there is more energy available for pre-emptive planning. Exploring the unique consequences of several alternatives can clarify the best path to take. This is what makes personal intuition so valuable. Even a tiny hint of trouble ahead can provide a timely warning for people who pay attention.

By carefully examining earlier training, events and circumstances, an individual can glean underlying causes for their recent decisions, current situations and likely future events. Sometimes, when burdened by old beliefs or repetitive negative experiences, people don't consider that a more desirable outcome is actually possible. One purpose for developing intuition is to examine our choices earlier, at a more leisurely pace, before urgent decisions are required.

When Erin arrived for a reading, she was concerned about her home renovation which was about to fall apart. A shy, softly spoken woman in her 60s, Erin was an infant-school teacher. She and her husband Brian were adding a granny flat to the back of the house so that her ageing mother Flora could live with them. Erin felt that having Flora close might benefit both of them.

Brian had been project-managing the building works but his explosive temper had already alienated their builder and electrician, who eventually refused to work with him. In a fit of pique, he wasn't prepared to manage the project any further and Erin was at her wit's end.

"We can't afford to hire a project manager and the job's less than half done. The roof is on but the windows aren't in and the electrical work isn't finished. I don't even know where we are with the bathroom and kitchen."

"Are you working right now?" I asked.

"No. I've just retired."

"Are you prepared to become the project manager for the rest of this development?"

"I couldn't do that. I know nothing about building. All I do is sign for deliveries and make coffee."

"Do you have to check each delivery before signing?"

"Yes, but that only takes a few minutes."

"This is part of project management on a small construction site like yours. All you'll be doing is extending your responsibilities and keeping your husband off-site so that the contractors can do their jobs without unnecessary interference."

Erin had several coaching sessions and some telephone meetings when urgent decisions were required. She hired an experienced builder, who took the time to explain each step to her. Erin spent most evenings searching the internet to understand the correct order for each step of the project while gradually learning about construction. It was a steep and sometimes stressful learning curve. I was happy to support her throughout the process, as her husband secretly hoped that she would fail. Knowing that he would gloat for years if she didn't complete the project was the motivation she needed to keep going.

Tension mounted at home, particularly when Erin suggested to her husband that she would manage the project. Brian scornfully scoffed at the idea. She phoned me that night, overwhelmed by the challenges ahead. I reminded her that Brian had already proven he couldn't manage the project without alienating everyone. It was now her turn to discover how smoothly a development can run when the project manager negotiates rather than shouts at tradespeople.

I reassured Erin that her competence would improve with experience and that she simply had to learn new skills. With the support of her experienced builder, the construction was eventually completed without any further bellowing. Flora loves her new home and is proud of her daughter's achievement. One added benefit for Erin is that Flora enjoys gardening. She's already planted an orange and a lemon tree, a lush hedge along the back fence and has plans for a kitchen garden. Fragrant early flowering jasmine is attracting bees and Flora is researching small fountains to attract bird life.

SIMPLE STEPS TO CHANGING YOUR DESTINY

Accepting that a goal is possible is the first step towards changing your personal destiny. Being comfortable with a desired outcome when it arrives is also essential. Limiting beliefs restrict our vision of possibilities.

Jessica felt that she was a long way from the life that she had painstakingly planned. An energetic, efficient woman, she arrived with a carefully prepared series of questions plus a second list of options.

With two young children, Jessica's days were busy but she was aware that in a few years they'd be at school and she would return to work. In particular, she wanted to study and forge a new career with better prospects than her previous administrative roles.

During her reading, she was disappointed when it seemed likely she would return to her old repetitive job. In a later coaching session, we considered some options for changing her destiny. Jessica seemed nervous about investing her time and energy in a university course because she fundamentally didn't believe that she was capable of completing it.

At 19, she commenced an arts degree at university, which she abandoned during her second year. Since then, she has been burdened with the belief that she is incapable of studying, despite having completed several short courses since.

We brainstormed different ways that Jessica could access support during her studies, including private tutors in her subjects, study technique coaching, hypnosis sessions for improved self-confidence and setting reviews to gauge her progress and determine where she might need assistance. The prospect of two long years of study stretching out before her seemed like an additional burden when added to her current home and family responsibilities.

Together, we explored the possibility of her enrolling in the course and taking each study block individually. During any semester break, she could postpone the course if she felt overloaded. In this way, she would be attempting four short courses on one topic. When she had completed them, she would earn a diploma and be ready for her new career direction.

I suggested a psychic reading at the end of her first year at university and again after completing her study, to gauge how much she had changed her life direction by taking the course and to encourage her forward. In this way, Jessica's commitment to study served two purposes. It would help her towards a more interesting career and show her that she has control over her own destiny. She was basically shifting from a fatalistic attitude to a more proactive, self-determined life.

"What happens if I feel overwhelmed and can't continue?" she enquired softly.

"Then, phone me and we'll re-examine your options."

"I could do that without phoning you."

"Yes, you could. However, if you believe that you have only one option, it's likely that you're not seeing other possibilities. My role is to remind you about your goals and help you to move forward towards them."

"Yes, but what if I'm exhausted by the children and I can't think clearly anymore?"

"If that happens, we'll consider ways to defer the course, get you more support with your children or more assistance with improving your study skills to make the process easier. You've told me that you want to climb this mountain and you know that it will require huge effort and commitment. If it was easy, you'd have done it already. It's important to remember that when you've reached this particular goal, other challenges are likely to be more achievable for you."

Together, we listed a range of small rewards for Jessica at the end of each semester. These included a full-body massage, a weekend away with two friends at their favourite country house hotel, or several days spent on her sofa watching DVDs while eating chocolate. At the end of the course, she would enjoy an afternoon shopping for new outfits for job interviews and dinner at her favourite seafood restaurant.

Jessica had some coaching sessions in the lead-up to her university course, plus several more throughout her studies. During these meetings, we focused on inhibitive childhood beliefs about her capabilities and personal limitations. Gradually, she began to realise that she was sufficiently skilled to successfully complete the course. As this happened, her anxiety slowly subsided and she was able to focus better on her studies.

When Jessica eventually completed her course with distinction, she had solid evidence that she was capable of doing it. Past experience builds confidence when facing future challenges. Next time she wants to undertake additional study she'll hopefully be more optimistic, especially when remembering her recent positive, personal experience. She'll know that it's possible for her to successfully accomplish her goals.

When Jessica abandoned her education earlier in life, her confidence diminished, particularly associated with study. Successfully completing a university course in her 30s restored her self-belief that she was capable of achieving her goals, especially as it didn't take her long to establish a suitable new career, where she is currently thriving. She emailed me during the pandemic to say that she was happily working from home and that she was grateful for the assistance. I reminded her that she had taken all of the steps herself — I was simply an observer.

When clients ask how they can change their futures to ensure better outcomes, each individual's path is unique. A clairvoyant can map out the milestones towards a more desirable outcome but sometimes people need additional help with specific steps. When they can successfully navigate the process without assistance, the new path is easily accomplished. However, when people stumble with one or more steps along the way, they're less likely to experience success. It's not impossible but without solid support and encouragement, the journey is more difficult. Everyone needs help at different stages, especially when tackling unfamiliar challenges. It doesn't matter if an individual plods or scurries towards an objective; perseverance is important.

Sometimes a path to success feels increasingly challenging and requires extra faith and persistence. Changing old, restrictive beliefs can force people to act with confidence while also acknowledging unique fears and doubts. When we're successful, it's important to celebrate our milestones—big and small—and regularly remember past personal achievements to continue forward momentum. Gradually, over time, our resistance subsides as confidence is reinforced.

To avoid early roadblocks, a clairvoyant can check to see if individuals need help to succeed or if they are capable of taking all of the required steps on their own. This forward trajectory isn't always foolproof.

Nathan, a regular client, took oppositional defiance to a subtle new level. He enquired about a job he had seen advertised, to determine if it might be suitable. When I told him that he would thrive in the position and grow with the company, he didn't even bother to apply for the opening. Once, he asked about the outcome of elective surgery. When I told him that it looked successful, his dark eyes softened with disappointment. It was as though I had given him bad news about his plans. He went home and cancelled the procedure immediately.

Nathan is unaware of the possibility that he's unconsciously obstructing his own progress. A small part of him desires change and wants to pursue opportunities, while a team of other parts actively sabotage his efforts to grow. It sometimes seems like the result of being cursed by an ancient God, whereby each day, he wakes up with the desire for change and hope fades by sunset.

In our last few clairvoyant readings, Nathan has resisted every path I have described for him. I wondered if, as a child, someone else had very firm plans about what Nathan should become, regardless of his own desires. As a result, resistance has become second nature to him. To test this theory, I'm tempted to advise him not to apply for a position I know he'll love, just to see how quickly he takes the job. However, my guides have suggested that I need to be very patient with him, as he needs gentle reassurance that he can change.

I've learned to ask two questions for every one Nathan asks. If he's interested in buying a new car, I ask, "Is this car suitable for Nathan?" and, "Will Nathan purchase this type of car in the next 12 months?" In this way, I can say that although the car is suitable, he's unlikely to buy it. I expect that, in time, he'll be ready to explore how past events have shaped his habit of self-sabotage. The fact that he sees options and asks for readings about life's possibilities suggests that the flame of hope is not entirely extinguished. My role is to avoid being dragged into this intimidating vortex of frustration, while nurturing his expectation that change is possible. Some days I feel like I'm sitting in the dark with Nathan, holding an unlit candle but unable to find any matches.

Despite his persistence, Nathan is stubbornly resistant to opportunities for growth and change. Perhaps because of childhood experiences, the path to any goal requires many more steps for Nathan than for other clients. These incremental stages allow him to become accustomed to change without experiencing any negative repercussions. Initially, his fear of negative consequences was so strong that he wouldn't even reach for new options. I gently reminded him that opportunities don't wait and many don't return.

Eventually, Nathan might be ready to embrace bigger steps in short periods when he has the capacity for that change. In the meantime, he's encouraged not to compare himself with others who may have experienced more positive upbringings. I tread a fine line between encouraging Nathan and reminding him that time is passing and that this is the youngest he'll be for the rest of his life.

I've seen enough people who, despite believing that change wasn't possible, eventually transformed and thrived. It wasn't easy but neither was enduring daily frustrations while knowing that they could be more than they had become. This has taught me that everyone can move closer to what they dream of becoming in life, especially with encouragement.

22. TRACING THREADS OF INFORMATION

In a recent telephone tarot reading, my client Inga was planning to buy her first home. She had found a perfect cottage that was to be auctioned on-site in four days. She asked if she would buy that property at auction on Saturday. The cards indicated that she wouldn't. She was disappointed but was relieved when I told her that she would purchase a suitable property in that suburb within four weeks.

She phoned ten days later to say that she had purchased her desired cottage, through a protracted negotiation, several days after the auction. The property didn't reach the vendor's target price, so it was unsold on the Saturday. I realised that the narrow focus of her question (buying the property on auction day) had resulted in a 'No' answer. If she had simply asked, "Will I purchase the property at number 12 Preston Avenue?" the answer probably would have been different. It's a subtle change, removing the Saturday time limit.

When searching for intuitive information, it can appear in the mind's eye as random scenes — a jumble of sounds, visuals, words or body sensations. With practice, by focusing on one specific image, it's easy to trace a thread that leads to a specific situation. It's like searching for a program on TV: scrolling down rows of pictures and pausing when something piques your interest.

With a TV, it's possible to click on a particular image and read more about the film, its actors and when it was released. To get the full experience, it is necessary to begin watching the movie. For people developing clairvoyance or visual intuition, this type of instant download is known as 'Uranian intuition'. It's an astrological term that refers to the unusual planet Uranus, the ruler of the sign of Aquarius. Uranian intuition is like downloading a whole file of information, such as a scene in a person's life, a set of circumstances, an event or the outcome of current efforts.

TYPES OF INTUITION

Lunar

Nocturnal dreams provide information about current circumstances, predict future events or reveal outcomes to allay fears. Often these details are interlaced with symbols or random moments from daily events and require decoding.

Intuitive dreams are sometimes like feature-length films, with every detail in glorious colour and whole stories packed tightly into a single sleep period. The dreamer is likely to wake up feeling tired and in need of a few more hours of rest but with vivid memories of the dream.

Neptune

Intuitive information pops into your mind when daydreaming, watching television or engaged in other activities. As it is unexpected, it can disappear as quickly as it arrives, making it difficult to tease out relevant details.

Neptune intuition is often sparked by a deep sense of compassion for others, surfacing when someone in need feels unable to request help.

Pluto

This involves gut feelings or instincts, especially about possible threats, secrets or hidden agendas. When furtive plans are sensed, it might require acute observation of a particular situation for a period of time to glean more information about covert activities.

Pluto intuition relies on personal suspicion to alert an individual to possible secrets. Then, with careful investigation and piecing together clues, it's possible to reveal what is being concealed. These people are persistent when teasing out more details from unwilling friends or strangers and are often discreet enough to seem only casually interested when asking probing questions.

As clairvoyants, Pluto people can be relentless when pursuing a thread of information, combining persistence with instinct to uncover hidden mysteries. Naturally secretive individuals are often uneasy around people with Pluto instincts, as they sense they are being scrutinised.

Uranus

Intuitive information (often visual) arrives as complete scenes, events or as likely outcomes. There is often more detail in each setting than is at first apparent and exploring a particular scene is like watching a part of a film repeatedly. This information can arrive like a flash from the blue. It is often unexpected and difficult to ignore. It's like downloading a file, complete with images and text.

Scenes appear suddenly and can disappear just as rapidly if ignored. It's as if the reader always knew about the person or subject that has only been in focus for 60 seconds.

Mercury

This involves thoughtfully designing a system for intuitive practice, such as meditation, before preparing careful questions that can steer intuition towards particular areas of life. These questions might focus on career, personal health, love relationships, creative talents and opportunities or family dynamics. It is a less creative, more systematic approach.

Mercurial intuition can provide a huge range of information but it can be difficult to narrow focus to glean more details about a particular person or aspect of an issue. Unlike the focused Pluto intuition, this is more conversational and a lighter, broader approach.

Sometimes in training sessions, I organise for a stranger to visit a class for 15 to 20 minutes. Their role is to be an unfamiliar client. All we know is the person's first name and age. We need to know their age to determine what is history (and likely to have already occurred) and what is yet to eventuate (and can possibly be altered). The only thing anyone can change about history is their perception of it. Everyone has free will to transform many parts of the future. If describing scenes to someone, I frame past events differently from future possibilities. When clients cannot confirm historical events (such as childhood situations), simply trace an intuitive thread to those circumstances to retrieve more accurate details.

Once, I was describing my patron Isabelle as a young girl visiting the circus with her aunt. She couldn't recall this event, so I traced the thread to the scene and described the gasps of the audience as balls of fire exploded before them while a pair of lions performed just metres from the crowd. Isabelle was spellbound at how the circus performers held the crowd's attention, surprising and delighting them in turn. The smells, sounds and visual performance seemed larger than life. This event planted a seed within Isabelle to become a performer. Soon afterwards, she took up gymnastics before giving it up later to pursue drama and dance lessons.

By providing Isabelle with more details from this particular event, she was able to recall this situation. She realised how this unique occasion in her past influenced her early desire to pursue acting.

Sometimes, despite tracing a thread and clearly describing a situation, a client is unable to relate to what is being said. When this happens, I simply move on to other scenes and information strands so that the session isn't consumed with a single, forgotten scene. Clients often confirm what has been described later, in an email or during subsequent readings.

TRACING THREADS

It's essential that the reader has an image, feeling, smell, taste or sound to work from at the beginning. I mention a range of senses because sometimes when I'm scanning a client's body for physical health issues, I experience a metallic or chemical taste in my mouth. I usually ask if the client is taking any heavy medications. Occasionally, I'll feel tightness in my throat, congestion in my chest or restrictive pain in the finger joints. These momentary sensations highlight issues in the client's own body.

It's much easier to trace threads of information if the initial glimpse is visual, because a lot of details are packed into a mental picture. By taking time to carefully examine the image in the mind's eye, the clairvoyant is effectively strengthening the intuitive thread to the client, where all other information is located. If the reader receives confirmation about what is being described, both participants usually relax and the psychic can access the client's information more easily. When people receiving predictive readings feel seen, heard and not censored, they are likely to be more open and present. If they don't need to filter what they are saying for fear of being judged, the entire intuitive process flows more smoothly.

While describing a mental image to a person, if a reader needs more information or the recipient asks a question about a specific area, simply return to the inner scene and then mentally move forward or back in time. Rita enquired about where she would meet her next long-term partner. I generally avoid this question because if a couple meet in an airport, taking a flight every week for the next 12 months won't necessarily speed up the meeting process but can lead to unnecessary frustration. In this instance, I decided to test it.

Tracing the first information thread, I glimpsed Rita at a wedding. She was standing outside a small church on a patch of lawn. Her attire suggested that she was part of the wedding party but she wasn't the bride. The groom stood a few metres away, talking to two other men. He turned and suggested one of them ensure that Rita was okay, as she was standing alone. Jacob walked over and smiled as he approached Rita. When she saw him approaching, she held her breath.

I mentally moved forward three hours to glimpse an image of Rita and Jacob at the wedding reception. They were seated at one of three long tables beneath a trellis that was covered in flowering wisteria. As wisteria flowers in spring, if it was an Australian wedding, Rita was likely to meet Jacob between late August and November. I then scanned out from the venue to see some of the cars parked in nearby streets. They had New South Wales number plates, so I assumed that this wedding was taking place in NSW, probably in Sydney.

Be careful with smaller details like car plates, as this wedding might take place in another state with many guests from interstate. Check more than one car's plate for improved accuracy. If possible, scan for a wedding invitation, as that's likely to include the venue address and the date. Sometimes a wedding invitation can be found on a table during the reception celebration.

With practice, it is possible to mentally rise above the wedding party and glimpse the suburb from above to gain more insight into the location. It's like a drone soaring above an event to gain a bird's-eye view. When more experienced with this process, it's easier to progress two, three and five years ahead to Rita's own wedding, to see if she marries Jacob.

The whole process begins with finding and exploring an initial thread of information. Once this is done, a connection to the person is established and more information strands become available. Some clairvoyants simply explore a range of threads throughout a reading but this approach might not answer the questions the client needs to ask. If a person asks a specific question, the reader can take a moment to search for an information thread related to that issue.

HOW TO TRACE INTUITIVE THREADS

1. Clear your mind. Take several deep breaths and concentrate only on your breathing.
2. Focus on the person's issue or question.
3. Notice what you sense.
4. Explain to the person what you can feel or see. If you have an image in your mind's eye, describe this carefully while exploring it slowly. Resist the temptation to interpret it because your perceptions of events might steer the client away from the actual meaning. If the scene is of the person relaxing in a comfortable home overlooking the ocean, don't assume that this is necessarily their home. It might be a holiday rental or a friend's house. Focusing on mental scenes before other sensations usually provides more details, resulting in faster recognition. Sometimes illuminating what you feel while witnessing the scene can also be valuable to the listener because it adds another dimension. If you feel excited for them or experience a sense of dread about an event or the outcome of a poor choice, this can alert the person to a positive or difficult life event.
5. Decide whether the images warrant more exploration. If so, expand your awareness to give the person more details. If not, let the scene go and repeat the process with new mental pictures and sensations.
6. Resist the temptation to over-interpret what you sense, as this can limit the listener's ability to recognise details. The impression you receive might have a different significance to the other person. A writhing snake might represent a threat to you, whereas the client might have a pet snake at home.
7. To improve your observation skills, look carefully. Scrutinise the scenes in your mind as you might if you knew that you'd later be called as a witness in court. If the images are fleeting, take a deep breath and release it slowly, letting go of outside distractions as you exhale. Then take a moment to focus all of your senses on the scene.

23. WORKING BACKWARDS FROM THE FUTURE

During pure clairvoyance readings, I intuitively scan back to past events in clients' lives or forward into likely future situations and circumstances. Often a person has asked about the outcome of a particular situation, such as a career opportunity, completion of current study or an overseas move. Having a specific question provides a point of focus.

When you know what you're looking for, such as an overseas move, it's easier to intuitively look ahead and land on that exact topic or concern. It's possible to scan forward with your focus on only one specific issue or area of life. This might be health, career, finances or the development of a young child in the family. By narrowing the focus as a reader, you're less likely to be distracted by other events or circumstances. This is not the same as looking ahead generally. It takes time and repetition to develop this skill. By pursuing every opportunity to practise the process, it's possible to improve your precision for when clients ask specific questions.

Marina explained that she was unhappy in her relationship and was considering returning to her homeland. She asked if she would go back to live in France. I scanned ahead two years to intuitively see her at home. The inside of her house was not enough to confirm her location, so I moved my perception of that image until I was above her small cottage, seeing it from the air. I was able to glance around to see a row of tiny terraced houses crowded down the hill to the sea below. This was obviously a European town, with cars parked on both sides of a one-way street. By shifting my focus down to a small group of shops nearby, I saw a sign that read 'Boulangerie'. I knew then that Marina was back in France.

This method of using intuition involves moving forward in time while focusing on the specific topic or query. The more precise the question, the easier it is to find relevant information.

In an open-ended career question such as, "'What does the future hold for my career?" there are several methods for gleaning information.

- Intuitively ask spirit guides to show the person's next job.
- Mentally scan ahead 12 or 24 months and describe what you can see in a usual workday.

This assumes landing on an average working day and if the described circumstances are new to the client, that this is their next job. When looking ahead and landing on a Sunday, simply move forward one day.

- Intuitively scan forward 10 years to have the (10-years-older) client tell you the outcome of their current career circumstances.

This requires rigorous practice to perfect but can be developed with persistence. You might ask every person you read for if you can try this for a few minutes at the end of each reading to simply improve your technique.

In one particular psychic development course, a student had recently applied for two positions with different companies and she wanted to know if she would be offered either job. I was demonstrating the 'Follow-the-Feet' exercise to a class at the time, so we tried it out together. This is a fun game where we mentally follow a client's feet into their home after the course and describe the furnishings and anything else we notice. (See Chapter 15 for more details of this exercise.)

In this instance, I instructed students to follow Kayleigh's feet 10 weeks ahead, at around 10:30 am on a Wednesday morning. If she accepted a new position, Kayleigh would be at her new workplace on that particular day. We chose a precise date so that we might all be looking ahead to the identical place at the same time.

The process initially involved guessing Kayleigh's footwear and clothing. Then, when we had identified her clothing (and warmed up to the process), we expanded our intuitive awareness to describe the room around her. Students were encouraged to state aloud what they saw and Kayleigh was asked to simply say "Yes" or "No". This is deliberate. A 'Yes' answer indicates that she recognises what has been described, while a 'No' suggests that she doesn't. A 'No' answer doesn't necessarily mean that the student is wrong but simply that Kayleigh isn't aware of those specific details. Each 'Yes' or 'No' answer is soon followed by another statement from a different person so that no one feels judged for a misstep.

I'm happy to go first and be wrong several times in a row to help students warm up to the idea that this is simply a game and that, eventually, someone will get the right answer. Sometimes they become rowdier than young children at a birthday party, laughing, rolling their eyes at suggestions and exuberantly shouting over each other.

Most of the information we were describing might not have been familiar to Kayleigh, as she had only briefly visited the company's offices for an interview. Kayleigh was saying "No" repeatedly during the process. That didn't stop the group, who were becoming more boisterous and enthusiastic as time passed.

In less than 10 minutes, we had clearly described the office of the second job she had applied for, including the views from various windows and her desk, plus her work colleagues. To test the process, I asked the group to move forward to 9 pm that evening. We accurately described Kayleigh's home, her cat and her partner, who was burning toast in the kitchen.

INTUITIVELY REVEALING LIFE OUTCOMES

If someone has a particular project to complete but is unsure how to arrive at the described conclusion, it's possible to intuitively ask to be shown some important decisions, actions and turning points leading to this eventuality. Then, ask if this is the best possible outcome and, if not, what needs to be done to bring about a more rewarding conclusion. This involves asking more questions, such as:

- What are the important decisions that will result in this outcome?
- What specific actions will lead to this goal?
- What are some crucial turning points likely to occur that will affect the outcome of taking this path?

Many people wish they had a chance to impart their current experience and wisdom to their younger selves, to diminish unnecessary pain and wasted time pursuing dead-end paths. However, this is only one side of a coin. The other is to contact our older, more experienced selves, perhaps 10 or 20 years into the future, to enquire about the wisdom of pursuing current goals.

In meditation, when the mind is still, with practice it's possible to contact one's higher self. This is the spiritual part of each person that has already seen the future, mastered the lessons and challenges and is well placed to advise the individual in the present day. (See higher-self meditation in Chapter 11.)

To minimise the risk of receiving bad news from your higher self, it's important to word questions carefully. Here are some possible questions:

- What do I most need to focus on right now in my life?
- What are some prospects ahead for me in the next year?
- How can I better prepare for life's opportunities before they arrive?
- What mental, emotional or spiritual burdens do I need to resolve or release to make the path ahead easier?
- How can I best deal with these issues?

- What are my strengths going forward?
- What areas within myself or my life do I currently need to improve?
- What skills do I require to make my life more rewarding?
- What choices for emotional nourishment do I have around me right now?
- What prospects for spiritual sustenance are available to me in the immediate future?
- What is the most suitable location for me to live in for the next stage of my life?
- Is there any pain that I have caused others that I need to atone for at this time?

It's tempting to ask about how life will be at the very end. We might reason that intuitively glimpsing the final days of this life can help give perspective to our current struggles and goals. How easily, though, can we accept the knowledge of unexpected events such as surviving a current spouse by 20 years, living alone after a bitter divorce or limited mobility resulting from a serious stroke? None of these events are likely to occur but there is a risk to knowing these harrowing details unless we feel empowered to avoid these outcomes. Be careful about asking long-term questions to avoid anxiety. It's generally better to ask a broad end-of-life question, such as, "What is my underlying purpose?" or, "Please describe some of the highlights of this life."

It requires great determination and careful planning to avoid arriving at an unwanted outcome, especially one you've intuitively glimpsed. It's not impossible but it is a daunting task. With power comes responsibility.

Using personal intuition to look ahead at your life over three or four decades can affect how much commitment you give to significant people and current goals. It's a rare individual who can make the most of every day in a current relationship, knowing that another long-term spouse will be arriving within several years.

If you have a burning desire to look ahead a long way, keep your focus broad. Some of the following questions might be suitable:

- What is the theme of my life?
- What is the underlying spiritual lesson for me in this lifetime?
- What skills or personal strengths do I need to develop for a more rewarding life?
- Show me some major opportunities available in the next 10 years.

None of the questions above are emotionally loaded. They provide images of the future, painted with broad brush strokes that won't leave people reeling. Glimpsing some of life's future opportunities allows us to better prepare to seize the day when it arrives. If an opening doesn't seem attractive, ask why this is significant. The answers are sometimes surprising.

LONG-TERM PREDICTIONS

When presenting long-term predictions for others, it's important to provide sufficient information to motivate people to climb their personal mountains without too much detail to minimise a sense of wonder at their summits. Few are confident of being happy with an outcome that is decades ahead, especially when we have no idea how the intervening years might shape us.

In its simplest form, the most dangerous question to ask a clairvoyant is, "When will I die?" The answer shadows the person, causing hesitancy around trust or inspiring recklessness when it's important to be careful. Everyone has a finite period of time but hasty or bad choices can end the journey prematurely.

Jenny's husband, John, died in his mid-fifties. The injustice of his early death, particularly when he was a fit man, haunted her. I initially thought that she simply felt cheated because they had planned a wonderful old age together and she suddenly found herself approaching retirement alone. However, closer scrutiny revealed that John was due to live another 12 years but his life was shortened because of a workplace accident 19 years earlier.

In his mid-thirties, John was a self-employed builder, renovating a suburban house he had purchased as a rental property. In the scene I glimpsed, the roof was off the home and the windows had been removed. A range of new windows was neatly stacked inside a room in preparation for installation. It had been raining but was now sunny. John hadn't planned to be on-site that day. He had stopped by briefly on his way home from an ocean swim. Without looking, he stepped back into a small puddle containing a fallen overhead power line and received an electric shock. He was immediately thrown into the air and landed on his back.

After a check-up at the emergency department, John went home and seemed fine. However, his heart had been weakened by the shock, and as a result, he died in his mid-fifties. His wife confirmed these events when I described them to her. She remembered collecting him from the hospital. I explained that it felt unfair because it was unplanned and unexpected. It had traumatically reshaped her life, leaving her to grieve alone and face a bleak old age without him.

This reading occurred years ago. If it happened today, I'd ask Jenny whether she would like to know what clarity she might derive from these circumstances to make the most of her time left here. It's easy to remind her that John will be waiting for her on the other side when she arrives but this might inadvertently reshape her destiny by preventing her from entering a new love relationship. She might feel that she would be cheating on her late husband.

Clairvoyants are guides who highlight routes to the summit without actually accompanying clients on these unique pursuits. An astute reader suggests what baggage such as grief, guilt, anger or resentment can be discarded to speed up the journey. The psychic can describe people who accompany the person for parts of the journey (in friendships or love relationships) and warn of major pitfalls to avoid along the way. However, a reader is not a sherpa. Pointing the way is not the same as traversing the path. We are simply map readers.

Experienced travellers usually carefully prepare before taking a journey that involves steep ascents and physical endurance. They strengthen themselves physically and research what is required for each stage of the journey. However, inexperienced hikers sometimes arrive at the base of a mountain with only summer clothing, wearing sandals and without even a torch, whistle or sunscreen. Readers often encourage clients to deliberately prepare for the journey they are taking. It's important to carefully suggest what might be required for safe passage to their personal summits.

One obstacle to clairvoyants being effective and helpful is that we only glimpse parts of a person's life. We have to advise clients without understanding exactly how steep the path they have taken has been, how past events have weakened or strengthened resolve and if the client's life compass is accurate or damaged. Unresolved past emotional upheavals can make current opportunities invisible. Experienced readers understand this and sometimes illuminate ways to heal these wounds on the path to fulfilment.

Some days I dream of designing a reading that determines how an individual might repair their personal life compass. Having an accurate scope is vital to finding a way home to spirit in the afterlife. When reading for clients who can't seem to function on a basic level—such as holding down a regular job or maintaining personal friendships—but who appear to be intelligent and resourceful, I'm aware of a damaged life compass.

As a reader, being able to steer someone with a deficient life compass towards a workable path to mend their inner orientation can be a powerful gift for that individual. Although the person might have years of therapy or spiritually cleansing pursuits ahead to resolve profound grief or searing rage, before charting a course towards true purpose, the journey has to begin somewhere. Initial steps are often small, producing barely noticeable progress as the individual develops skills that become positive habits for life.

People with accurate bearings for direction and purpose can help fellow travellers by gently pointing the way — not necessarily up the mountain but towards repairing their inner alignment and orientation. This allows an individual to chart a unique, meaningful path in life. Meditation or regular contemplation are some of the fundamental ways to heal past pain. This process also helps refocus someone away from revenge or bitterness, towards spiritual purpose and a meaningful life. It's sometimes easier to accept life's obstacles or setbacks when there is a fundamental understanding of your deeper life's purpose.

Sometimes, people become stuck because of the unfairness of their situations. When this happens, it's necessary to remind them that it isn't fair what has happened. Waiting for life to be equitable is often a fruitless pursuit that consumes decades, sometimes swallowing every day that remains after a trauma. It isn't right that, after a deep upheaval, a person has to heal, grieve, accept the setback and then resume living, sometimes missing years in the process. This can mean that they have to mourn lost years too, when friends were travelling the globe, enjoying career advancement, meeting new partners and buying homes. Comparison with others can make people bitter, especially if one suffers a huge setback while others sail on calm seas throughout life. In these readings, it's worthwhile to intuitively move ahead to the person's final day, to discover the underlying lesson or the strengths they need to develop to move beyond past pain. It can give the individual a meaningful objective to aim for in life.

24.
ASTRAL TRAVELLING

When the physical body falls asleep at night, the astral body (one of the finer energy bodies) is free to slip away. It can move up through the ceiling and across the neighbourhood to reunite with friends. Occasionally, it travels to meet deceased friends or relatives, particularly recently departed loved ones. This can help people to process grief and loss after a recent death.

Sometimes, we clearly recall what this energy body has experienced when we wake up. But often, all awareness of the astral body's trips is lost upon awakening. It's possible to train yourself to recall more of what you experience on the astral plane by simply asking yourself to remember before going to sleep at night.

IMPROVING MEMORY OF ASTRAL TRAVEL AT NIGHT

- As you fall asleep each night, simply state to yourself, "Tonight, I will remember what my astral spirit body experiences while I'm asleep and I'll recall this clearly tomorrow."
- Keep a pen and pad, or a digital tablet, handy to write down basic details first thing in the morning.
- Be persistent with the process, as it can take more than five weeks to experience regular results. Fundamentally, you are asking your conscious mind to connect more closely with your subconscious, to perform complex actions. Like any new skill, it takes time and practice to become skillful with the method.

- If you feel repeatedly overwhelmed or insufficiently rested when you wake up, discontinue this exercise. Restful sleep is essential to mental health and wellbeing and is more important than remembering night-time travels. This is simply an interesting exercise. It can be used for information retrieval of nocturnal sojourns and provide awareness of those parts that don't need rest or sleep at night.
- If you still want to remember your night-time astral adventures, use this technique only once or twice a week, to reduce interference with refreshing sleep and deep rest.
- When experienced with the process, it's possible to recall visiting friends, exploring other locations or attending sleepers' classes. (These are opportunities for learning that involve only slumbering individuals.)

Sometimes elderly people, who have been ill for a period and are approaching the end of their lives, travel off to a meeting point on the other side. Deceased friends or relatives can meet and reassure them that they'll be fine once they have released their physical bodies. It's a chance to explore the next life with familiar guides, just the way a mother might take a small child to visit her first school several weeks before lessons begin.

With practice, it becomes easier to consciously astral travel while awake. This requires patience and persistence, as it can be a complicated process. Robert Monroe has written about this in-depth in his books *Journeys Out Of The Body* and *Far Journeys*.

Regularly consuming alcohol and some medications can interfere with the memory of astral travel. The astral body travels each night anyway, as it's not trapped in the physical body when a person sleeps. People who are on antidepressants, tranquilisers or some psychiatric drugs usually experience less intuitive sensitivity as a result of these.

Strong medicines can also affect dreams at night and their influence varies with the products consumed. Sometimes, medicines reduce dream recall, and occasionally, people wake up with vivid memories of the wildest dreams imaginable.

Even when students begin to recall their dreams each morning, it takes skill and patience to determine what are attempts by the subconscious mind to sort through recent daily experiences and what are genuine astral travel events. If you're not sure, an astral travel partner might help. If you can find someone to partner with you for a few weeks, each night before sleep, you can plan to visit each other during the night. First thing after waking up, each participant writes down any interaction remembered that night involving both people. This can also be saved on a voice recorder or phone. Every couple of days, check with each other to gauge if both of you experienced similar experiences at night.

When burdened by daily demands and responsibilities, the astral body is glad to escape its physical constraints at night. It is a welcome relief to slip away from constant worry, anger, sorrow, guilt, regret, or time spent experiencing profound spiritual hunger. For a few hours each night, this etheric body can travel free from gravity, time, the need to remain within a safe temperature range or physical hunger and thirst. It can search for sources of nourishment, knowledge, or spend time with distant friends.

One of the benefits of conscious astral travel or remembering where you've been at night can occur when a person has an important meeting the next day. Sometimes the astral body slips out to visit the location of a planned job interview or the café where a person has arranged to have coffee with someone they've recently met online.

Several years ago, I received an email from a European author of a series of tarot books, who was visiting Sydney and wanted to catch up for lunch. We hadn't met before but my first tarot book was used as course notes by some teachers he worked with in his home city. I was a bit surprised to receive his email as we had not met before.

On the day of our lunch meeting, I arrived at the location and he was already seated.

The surroundings felt familiar and when he handed me a tarot book and deck he had designed, I wasn't surprised. It occurred to me that I had visited the location and him during sleep before we met in person, to ensure that there were no hidden agendas. I was impressed by his unique tarot deck, realising that it had probably taken more time to design than to actually write the book.

If a person has an important meeting, job interview or significant event approaching, especially in a location they have not previously visited, it makes sense to visit the venue to gauge how far it is from public transport or the best entrance to use. Most times, an individual does this during sleep the night before an event and promptly forgets it upon awakening. Developing personal intuition is a process of observing, listening and sensing the smoothest way forward.

If all it takes is five minutes during sleep to discover a suitable nearby car park for a busy venue, then it's useful. Yes, you can use an app to find a car park but probably not to scan the interior of an office where an interview will take place. Being able to familiarise yourself with the venue can help you feel more relaxed on the day of the meeting or interview.

CONSCIOUS ASTRAL TRAVELLING

Conscious astral travel while asleep at night requires practice and training to assist with remembering each experience upon awakening the next morning. Although the physical body requires sleep at night to rest, repair itself and have a break from the stress of worldly demands, spirit forms don't need respite.

While the physical body sleeps at night, the astral form leaves to enjoy several hours of freedom. This is liberation from the restrictions of gravity, temperature and the laws of physics. The astral parts of people who are spiritually asleep in their lives usually sit on the end of the bed or remain inside the room or the home where the physical person is resting.

The astral parts of individuals who are spiritually awake often make the most of this period of freedom to travel off to visit friends, explore other locations, attend classes or consult guides or spiritual masters. When the physical form needs to turn over, reposition itself or wake up, it summons the finer spiritual bodies so that it can move.

On rare occasions, the physical body sends out a message to the astral part and then wakes up before the astral form has returned. When this happens, the individual is momentarily paralysed in the physical form for a few seconds until the astral body returns. Sometimes it can take up to several minutes for the astral form to return, which is very stressful for the person who cannot move.

In the 1980s, I employed experienced people to teach psychic development courses, and sometimes, I'd meet them after classes and discuss the process. One teacher, Toby, was keeping a diary of paired meditations with a man in India. Despite being a long distance apart physically, they met remotely twice a week in meditation and practised techniques together. Toby explained that this had been going on for several months but they had never met or even spoken to each other in real life.

Toby, a keen traveller, sometimes goes to bed early to extend the time he has to travel at night during sleep. He explores towns and cities remotely before planning his next overseas trip so that he knows which parts of each country he'll enjoy the most. Then he buys tickets and visits physically.

Sometimes, when out travelling at night, Toby enjoys sitting in on a talk delivered by a master or attending group meditation in Thailand. One morning, I received a phone call from him to say that he was unable to teach his usual Tuesday evening class. I laughed and explained that he had already visited me the previous night and told me while I was asleep.

"Oh, that's great. I wasn't sure you'd remember, so I thought it best to call you."

25.
MEETING YOUR LIVING MASTER

If you're unable to contact your living spiritual mentor in meditation, it's possible that they will visit you during sleep at night. If so, those particular experiences usually seem sharper and more clearly defined, as well as more memorable than other nocturnal dreams. Sometimes, inexperienced meditators despair at not being able to meet their guides or spiritual mentors in meditation. We have all been assigned to a particular master, so it is their responsibility to contact us and guide us on our paths. This doesn't always have to occur in meditation. It can happen during a long walk out in nature or an afternoon of watercolour painting.

Meeting your own living master is a powerful emotional experience, especially if you feel misunderstood by friends, family or co-workers. Sensing empathy and compassion from another person for your journey can feel overwhelming. It's not unusual to cry or laugh joyfully during these meditative encounters when reminded of the best parts of yourself.

These meetings can yield intense sources of spiritual and emotional nourishment, providing strength to forge ahead with personal intuitive and spiritual development. Sometimes after contacting a living master, it's natural to want to help others as the meeting leaves you feeling abundantly nurtured. Students often describe feeling that they are very clear about their personal life direction as well as what is important in life after such profound meditations.

Some people discover their living spiritual mentor when a friend gives them a book by that master or they attend a talk or a group meditation by the person. Others attend lots of different groups in search of the teacher that resonates with them. When meeting an inspiring mentor that's not your living spiritual teacher, you'll experience the pure energy radiating from that person but not necessarily sense a profound connection.

When meeting your living master, if you pay attention, there is often a sense of coming home or reigniting a relationship with a long-lost friend. Some people never physically meet their living spiritual teachers, making all contact through dreams, books, group meditations, astral travel or private meditation. This can be equally effective because spiritual teachers can provide guidance from a distance while their students take unique paths through life.

Recorded talks by a living master or written materials, including books or shorter pieces, can provide a deeper understanding of that individual's particular philosophies. These are often available where spiritual pilgrims meet to meditate, especially if everyone at the meeting place shares the same living master. The added benefit of group meetings is the support and encouragement from fellow travellers, who often face the same obstacles. Being among like-minded people is a valuable source of nourishment and increases resolve when difficulties arise. Group members also demonstrate how to maintain a balance between physical world demands and spiritual needs. They are essentially your spiritual family, united by divine paths and long-term objectives.

26. THE AFTERLIFE

In some pure clairvoyance readings, I intuitively move forward to the client's last day to mentally ask them to tell me:

- the highlights of the life recently lived.
- the themes of that existence.
- the underlying spiritual lesson for the current lifetime.

I then progress forward to see who meets the person when they arrive in the hereafter. People are usually met by parents, family members, partners or close friends who have pre-deceased them, before being taken to meet a host of other deceased relatives.

Sharon appeared listless when she arrived for a reading. At first, I wasn't sure if she was exhausted or heavily medicated. She needed clear instructions to be repeated several times, as her attention and awareness were fuzzy.

Sharon explained that her relationship of 10 years had ended after a health diagnosis. A genetic test had recently confirmed that she had inherited an illness that was likely to end her life in her early 50s. Her father, his parents and his siblings had all died in their early 50s and this likely possibility was overwhelming for Sharon's partner Peter, who left her.

Although feeling compassion for Sharon, it was possible to also see Peter's viewpoint. If they had children together, Sharon might be gone before they reached 21 and he would be left grieving the loss of his wife while raising teenagers. It was as though an enormous, black cloud had settled over her life and ended a positive relationship. It initially seemed very unfair, partly because glimpsing the bigger picture proved difficult.

I looked ahead to see that Sharon was unlikely to see her 54th birthday and that when she died, Peter would be there in the afterlife to meet her. Although he was terrified that his life partner might only live a short time, it never occurred to him that his life might be shorter than hers. I saw that he had died suddenly in a car accident in his 40s.

My guides indicated that it was okay for me to tell Sharon this. I wasn't sure how to approach it, so I explained that when her life ended, Peter might be there to meet her. Sharon was shocked. I then explained their opening conversation in the hereafter.

"Peter explained that he had picked out a home for the two of you to share. You immediately say, 'Oh no,' because you're concerned about his personal taste."

"He has terrible taste! Absolutely awful," she agreed, laughing.

"What he means is that he wants to resume over there what you could not complete in this life."

"How long will I have to wait to be with him again?" she asked, tears streaming down her face.

"Suddenly, going home early doesn't seem so bad?" I said and she laughed. It was as though all of the goalposts had been moved, the rules of the game had been changed and there was to be a long break between the first and second half.

Fortunately, Sharon was an emotionally strong person, who, in the moment, was able to eventually see the bigger picture I had described. It was a reading that began with a simple question, "Will our relationship resume soon?" and ended with more information than the client expected to hear. It was more than I anticipated telling her and these were not necessarily details I'd divulge to another, more vulnerable person.

Realising that Peter wasn't coming back soon, Sharon asked about her next possible relationship. It was going to be challenging to be in the moment with a new partner while a part of her effectively waited for Peter. It was sad to see him make this enormous decision based on limited information, yet remaining together might have led to their children losing both parents before becoming adults. There was love ahead for both of them and Sharon's new partner was likely to have one child with her.

WHEN READINGS REVEAL LESSONS

Sometimes, both the clairvoyant and the client are surprised at what surfaces in a reading. It is a powerful moment when discovering the life theme or underlying spiritual path for the present lifetime. These lessons are often only a single word, while also being a lifetime's challenge. Telling clients that their decades spent here are to learn about deep trust, forgiveness, seizing joy or pursuing an idea relentlessly, often provides a life focus.

Sometimes, when individuals reach the afterlife following a prolonged illness or a period of loneliness in old age, they quickly revert to an early time in their recent existence when life was more rewarding or full of promise. In one reading, Miriam's mother, Betty, had passed over not long before. When I saw Betty, I was surprised that she looked as though she was in her mid-twenties, not her late 80s. Miriam explained that Betty had been lonely at the end and simply wanted to join her deceased husband and many of her departed friends. This also occurs when a person is confined to a wheelchair later in life. They'll frequently return to a time when they felt fit and active.

Occasionally, a person doesn't naturally release the recent life, particularly if this world has people who desperately miss the deceased. A mother of young children, or a daughter of an ageing parent who pre-deceases that parent, can feel an obligation to remain close to the physical world to help those left behind. As a clairvoyant, it's sometimes emotionally overwhelming to learn about lives interrupted but it's essential to remain impartial as people are often too close to events to glimpse life's bigger picture.

In a reading, Heather appeared agitated, unable to release someone and move on with her life. She explained that her partner had died unexpectedly two years previously, possibly from suicide. When I traced an information thread it seemed that he was engaging in risky behaviour and lost his life. He was experimenting with strong drugs, flirting with death without realising that it's a permanent state once that line is crossed. He was shocked when he collapsed and died. He became consumed with regret at the life they wouldn't share together and their carefully prepared plans that wouldn't be fulfilled.

Desperate to hold on to the life he had lost, Hank was still lingering around Heather, day and night, and she sensed this. As a result, it was more difficult for her to release him and embrace life again. Despite sensing his despair, I had to explain to his spirit that he had taken a risk and lost his life as a result. He needed to move on now and not interfere with Heather's destiny. He reluctantly agreed with this, especially when I highlighted how he was only more lonely and emotionally hungry since he passed over. Happiness for Hank required that he move on to those who awaited him in the afterlife. He would meet Heather again when she passes over, decades from now.

When Heather returned for a reading several years later, she seemed more relaxed. Her questions in that session revolved around Troy, her new partner. Life goes on. Heather didn't forget Hank but she couldn't waste her precious remaining years pining for him.

WHY THE DECEASED VISIT LIVING LOVED ONES

It's natural for departed people to return to visit friends or family members, usually meeting them in sleep at night, when the physical body is resting and the spiritual body is more open to visitors. Although the mind and body need daily rest, spirit bodies don't. While sleeping at night, the spirit being slips away from the weary physical frame. During this time, this part of the person is available if deceased friends or relatives visit.

This frequently occurs repeatedly following death for up to six months, after which time the departed are encouraged by those on the other side to move on and leave this world. Sometimes a deceased friend or relative will visit annually on an important date, such as a birthday or a wedding anniversary. Very close departed friends are usually present to receive the new arrivals after death, the way friends might meet expected visitors from overseas at an airport. Reunions are often joyful moments, even when the person has died unexpectedly.

After that first year, the recently departed visit less often. This is sometimes because their living friends are no longer holding on to them or missing them constantly, or they are more focused on opportunities on the other side.

When being met by a few close friends or relatives, the recently deceased are usually taken to meet other departed friends, relatives and ancestors. Occasionally, one or two of those in the crowd will be confined to a chair or still carrying scars from a physical life. This is often the result of that individual not believing in being free to discard the old world upon entering the new.

VISITING THE DECEASED IN DREAMS

It's possible to consciously visit departed friends during sleep at night. This process requires practice and perseverance, whereas the unconscious approach only requires that you set an intention to visit someone in particular. Your traveller body can do this while you sleep. The part of this activity requiring practice involves remembering and writing down what took place when you visited the afterlife. The self-suggestion as you fall asleep at night is as follows. You tell yourself (aloud or in your mind):

- Tonight, I want to visit Elsie, wherever she is now.
- I want my spiritual sight to be my physical sight so that I remember what I have seen in the morning.
- Tomorrow, when I recall my visit to Elsie and others, I'll write it down.

It can take up to a month of trying the process to consciously remember your nocturnal travels and up to a month or more for some people. Persistence is key. Don't bother on nights when you've consumed alcohol or taken medication to sleep, as this interferes with the process.

For me, this visiting process occurs in dreams at night. A good friend of mine, Caroline, passed away suddenly when she fell down the stairs at home several years ago. She lived in London, and when I stayed with her during extended visits to the UK, she took me away on weekend tours to show me the small towns of England. We originally met in Sydney when she lived here for a few years in the 1980s. We had so much fun on our weekend jaunts as she was bold, cheeky — and, being single, very quick to notice any available man in a crowd.

In my dreams that followed Caroline's death, I visited her and we went touring as we had in times of old but at the end of each dream, she reminded me that I couldn't stay. I was upset at leaving her but this eventually settled with time. More recently, we caught up briefly and she explained how she had moved on from her original lodgings to a new home (a higher spiritual plane). In these dreams, I know that I'm just visiting an old friend who has landed on her feet after a lonely and gruelling end of life.

I'm wondering where she'll insist that we visit for a weekend when I finally arrive for good.

One night during an astral visit, Caroline laughed when she remembered how I fell asleep face down in my salmon salad a few hours after a 23-hour flight. She had collected me from Heathrow Airport and I talked excitedly during the car journey home. She set a table in the soft sun on the deck and went inside to answer the phone, only to return and discover me sleeping soundly, with a face full of salad. My nickname was Salad Face for the rest of the trip. She even booked lunch for two at a café under that name. When we arrived, she loudly announced to the greeter, "Salad Face; table for two at 1 pm."

VISITING DECEASED FRIENDS THROUGH MEDITATION

It's also possible to meet deceased friends or relatives in meditation. When Inga booked a pure clairvoyance reading, she wanted to contact David, her late husband. David had died five months before the session at age 38 and Inga was experiencing profound grief at his passing. During the main part of the reading, I barely mentioned David. However, when Inga specifically asked about him and explained that he had recently died, I intuitively went searching for him.

"Did he take his own life?" I asked, seeing a man who'd endured a difficult existence and was agitated, in a state of emotional chaos during the final hours of his life. She confirmed that he had. When people suicide, it's often more difficult to reach them on the other side. I simply ask my guides to relay information between us so that I'm not swept up into any residual feelings of anger, grief or loss the departed spirit is experiencing.

I explained to Inga that David's spirit had visited her daily throughout the first four weeks after his death but that his helpers on that side had instructed him to pull back and focus instead on clearing all the pain and emotions from his recent life. I was informed that he would need another 12 to 14 months to clear everything, after which he could return to revisit Inga.

Soon after that, David would be instructed to refrain from visiting Inga, to avoid influencing her free will as she lived her life without him. Looking back to the weeks following David's death, I intuitively saw that his spirit visited Inga frequently but his anxiety, guilt and pain about ending his life only burdened her. He was effectively interrupting and prolonging her challenging healing process.

I looked ahead to see who'd meet Inga on the other side when she eventually arrived (in around 30 years). Her grandmother was there, along with a future husband who'd pre-deceased her. For the first time, she saw David without his anxiety, chaos and confusion. She saw him as a focused, clear-eyed man who was pleased to see her again.

Part of the reason for David being instructed to step back and let Inga live her life was to allow her to meet two new potential husbands without feeling as if she was betraying him. If he remained strongly connected to her, there might be karmic consequences for him steering her life in a particular direction. Another reason to release Inga was because David would eventually move further away from the physical world, making it more difficult to return. He needed to pursue his existence independently while Inga continued her life in the physical world.

Releasing your life left behind is essential when a person passes over because there is nothing anyone can do to retrieve this life once it's gone. The desire to hold on to those memories recedes as spirits of the deceased gracefully release their lives, particularly people who suffered ill health in their final years. Having a pain-free spirit body that doesn't require medication, food, or sleep is a wonderful relief. Pain and ill health are usually discarded with the physical body after death. Rarely an individual holds on to an illness or a physical disability after death, usually when this has defined that individual throughout life.

In one reading, I described a client's father as a tall man who strode around impatiently. When they met in the afterlife, he took his son to his abode and I was surprised to see a walking cane hanging on a coat rack. My client confirmed that as a result of an injury, his deceased father had used a cane in later years. "He won't need it when you meet him next," I explained.

When people have lived long lives but endured physical discomfort or loneliness prior to death, their spirits often return to times in that existence when life was more bountiful. This might be to an age when they had many opportunities and few responsibilities, perhaps in their teens or 20s. When reading for clients with deceased parents, they sometimes don't immediately recognise them from the descriptions given because they might not remember the person at that age. Who wants to shuffle around as a 91-year-old when they can simply choose to be 25 again?

DIFFICULTY ESTABLISHING CONTACT

During a pure clairvoyance reading, when attempting to contact someone who is deceased, I ask for them and if they are not accessible for any reason, I don't force the issue. It's the same in meditation. If I want to meet someone on the other side who is unavailable that day, I return at another time.

When someone has been departed for several years, it's sometimes difficult to establish contact. This is partly because they might have progressed up a few levels or spiritual planes, taking them further from this physical world. They return to meet friends when they arrive on that side; however, it requires more effort from them to reach the physical world. In some readings, a parent who has been gone for 20 years is ready and waiting when a client arrives for a session. In these instances, it's likely that this parent has met the client in dreams at night to arrange a more conscious meeting.

Sometimes being a clairvoyant can be tricky. This is particularly so when I intuitively see several deceased partners ready to meet a person on the other side, especially if that individual has not yet met these partners in real life and is still happily married to their first spouse. When this occurs, I usually say, "You'll have three chances for marriage in your life." When presented as opportunities, the additional potential spouses become a self-affirming benefit instead of a threat to current stability and happiness. Although the client is contented now, they might happily divorce one or more of those spouses when circumstances change.

WHEN A SPIRIT TAKES OVER COMMUNICATION

Contacting the deceased on behalf of the living provides people with important information to help them resolve past issues and focus on future opportunities. Tread softly when approaching the departed, as it's not the right of the living to interrupt the deceased. It's also considered trespassing when those who have departed attempt to influence the living.

Lisa initially consulted me because Dalia, a deceased friend, took control of her readings when Lisa consulted her regular medium. Lisa was unable to communicate with her late mother because Dalia took over the session, just as she had frequently dominated conversations during her life. Dalia was a determined person, always ready to tell her friend Lisa what to do. Dalia had strong views on Lisa's partner and her boss and was quick to mention her weight gain while Lisa was grieving her recently deceased mother. I was surprised that the medium didn't establish stronger boundaries with Dalia's spirit but perhaps she would have done this if Lisa had spoken up. When I have a deceased spirit who insists on being heard for an entire reading, I usually ignore this being after a few minutes to allow for other issues and questions to be discussed.

It's important to remember that because someone has died, they haven't suddenly become enlightened. Deceased spirits, especially those that are more attached to the earth plane, are strikingly similar to the people they were in their most recent lives. They still display the same interests, character traits and many of the prejudices they had in life. This lack of perspective can bias them when they pass on messages to living loved ones.

CONTACTING A SPIRIT THAT IS LONG GONE

When contacting a deceased loved one who has been gone for a year or more and is likely to have released the earth plane, messages passed on are less influenced by that spirit's recent life. Some individuals discard their earthly experiences moments after physical death, as though life was just a long dream and they are now awake again. Others hold on for years, gradually becoming weary and frustrated that they cannot exert influence in the physical world.

When intuitively glimpsing life summaries, it's possible to observe talents, strengths and character traits that flow through families, meaningful trips taken through the person's life, the arrival of each child and often grandchildren not yet in this world. Sometimes you witness conquest after struggle, hopes and plans abandoned or relationships and responsibilities that derailed an individual from an intended path in life. It becomes obvious what has shaped a person. If someone's plans were abandoned due to life demands, this individual might regress after death, to a time when goals were still possible and hope had not yet been extinguished. It's a way to remember a person's life more positively.

27. CONTACTING THE DECEASED

For many people, the finality of the death of a loved one is overwhelming. Accepting that you will never again see that person in your lifetime is almost unbearable. The survivor struggles with pain and despair but life goes on. There are two basic schools of thought regarding mediumship or contacting the deceased. Before examining the merits of each, it's important to understand why people contact the dead.

While experiencing deep sorrow and loss, a grieving person realises that eventually, he or she will die along with all other friends, family and acquaintances. If this person has children, it's possible to be dimly remembered in the DNA of descendants never met. During the initial period of mourning the loss of a loved one, many people search for answers. Unable to accept that their friends have gone forever, they sometimes seek solace in religion, in past and future lives or in consulting a medium who can contact the deceased on their behalf.

A medium is a conduit between this world and the next. Usually, when professional mediums are self-taught or discovered their abilities suddenly, there has been a death or a deep loss preceding the 'opening up to spirit'. The burning desire to see a lost friend or a deceased child one more time can result in 'breaking through' into the place where the deceased initially reside. It's only where they rest immediately after death because, in time, most deceased people move further away from physical realms as they continue their spiritual journeys.

Some people believe that it is not wise to disturb the deceased and that individuals have no business on that side of the veil (until we die). Moreover, they believe that the deceased are not meant to revisit the living until they are born with a physical body. In some particular religions and spiritual organisations, disturbing the dead is frowned upon as they believe that selfish people may end up demanding too much of those who have passed over, instead of taking personal responsibility for their own lives.

When Kyle's mother died, he consulted a medium to ask her what to do about his workplace issues and if he should quit his job. At age 46, he was still living in his childhood home and allowing his mother to make decisions for him. Although the medium encouraged Kyle to take control of his life, it was easier to ask his mum.

It's important to remember that if a person regularly consults a medium to contact a friend or relative years after that friend has passed over into spirit, it's likely that the contacted spirit has not progressed from the lowest realm or level. This can occur when a person dies with no spiritual awareness or the spirit has a strong attachment to the physical world. As a result, the information provided is unlikely to be any more valuable than if your ageing uncle had moved overseas and you phoned him periodically for advice.

Others think that it is okay to contact the deceased in a respectful manner for reassurance, clarity about life issues, or to simply know that you have not been forgotten. I believe it is fine to contact the departed if and when they are available.

In the six weeks following a death, the deceased might visit loved ones to reassure them that everything is okay. This is often done during sleep, when the spiritual body is out of the physical body. It can be difficult for grieving people to notice the spirit of a person who has recently passed when they are overwhelmed, depressed or struggling with everyday life.

When this occurs, the visited sometimes describe waking up crying with pain and joy, or awakening with a jolt to the clear sound of the deceased person's voice. Often, they'll describe the smell of the person's fragrance or cologne lingering in the room afterwards. This may be an aftershave, a perfume, the smell of cigarettes if that person was a smoker or simply the unique body smell of that particular individual.

Gradually, those who have passed over visit less, mainly on anniversaries or birthdays. If there is a strong bond, they are present when close friends die, to welcome them and show them the way forward. When elderly or terminally ill people are dying slowly, they sometimes describe dreaming of deceased relatives. The living person is usually astral travelling to visit departed friends or relatives during sleep at night. It's a chance to visit their next destination a few times before moving on permanently.

SAFETY GUIDELINES

There are a few safety guidelines around contacting the dead. Opening yourself up to meeting any deceased person is like offering a ride to a complete stranger on a dark country road at night. It's possible to enjoy a great conversation or end up as a police statistic. Remember that if old Joe was a handyman for 50 years before he died, he's likely to be more interested in telling you how to fix your back gate than how the universe works. Being without a physical body hasn't suddenly made him a spiritual master.

Some ambitious people aim higher when wanting to contact the departed, compiling a list of deceased seers, lamas, teachers and ascended spiritual masters, to boost their CV.

Wanting to contact a deceased prophet is a difficult process, even for experienced meditators. This is because the more spiritually evolved a person was in life, the higher the spiritual plane he or she will reside on. It's difficult to reach higher planes without specific techniques that involve temporarily discarding all of your lower energy bodies. It's like climbing a very tall mountain. Towards the summit, the air thins out and many climbers struggle for sufficient oxygen. They discard all but the most vital possessions, as everything they carry suddenly seems to weigh more.

I described this releasing process in my book, *A Secret Door to the Universe*, where my teacher, Christine, helped me to do this in meditation. The procedure was like leaving behind my character, emotions, ambitions and identity, leaving only the finest spiritual bodies. It was as though I had been stripped down to pure light. For the next few months in 1992, I was still in that light when I wrote the book long-hand. It was a taste of being pure light, without a spiritual body, and I—despite regular meditation—haven't experienced it since.

It is essential to implement a method of cleansing and protection before, during and after each attempt to contact the departed. This is to avoid lost souls attaching themselves to you as a source of light. This can occur with people who passed away without strong spiritual beliefs. A fear of the unknown or a desire to remain on Earth can prevent the spirit of the recently departed from moving forward. Instead, their energy body remains temporarily trapped between this world and the next.

When someone meditates and cleanses with spiritual light before venturing out to discover and commune with the dead, the trapped energy body sees the light and believes that this is a way home to an intended resting place. Instead of going forwards, the energy body becomes attached to the person meditating, and if not carefully removed, can remain with that individual until death. Someone very experienced with spiritual cleansing can carefully release these attached bodies. However, be careful. Most people who believe that they can do this work are usually only imagining that they can.

In 1991, during my studies in the UK and in Greece, my teacher Christine was very clear about this point. She explained that unless you have been over to the other side and you know your way around the afterlife (the spiritual realms), don't attempt soul-rescue work. It's complicated and if your inner light is stronger than the person you are cleansing, the entwined spirit is likely to attach itself to you. If this occurs, the habits, routines and beliefs of that particular energy body might influence you for the rest of your days. It could become a prolonged negative experience.

If you doubt your ability to protect or cleanse yourself, find an accomplished medium to contact the deceased on your behalf. Don't be tempted to step into deep water without a life jacket, especially without a lifeguard in sight. Rips are a common factor for novices and often catch them unaware. Experienced mediums are usually familiar with the risks involved and often have solid protection mechanisms to deal with attached entities.

One method of contacting the departed involves meditating and requesting the deceased person by name. This might be the name provided by the client or the one the person was known by throughout their recent life. The strength of this technique is that it's similar to contacting guides or your higher self. It's an extension of a familiar method.

Another process involves vacating your physical body to allow the spirit of the deceased to briefly enter it and have a conversation with the client. This involves more risk, such as becoming exhausted by the process and vulnerable to a lifeforce that doesn't want to leave your body or wants to return at will when you are not receptive. It's wise to only attempt this method in a group environment, with an experienced team of mediums who can keep time and rescue you if issues arise with returning to your physical body. This method is not recommended for inexperienced people and is unnecessary. You can meet the deceased and retrieve information without surrendering your personal space, so there's no tangible benefit from allowing an unfamiliar energy body to have free rein over your physical body.

In circumstances where I sense that it's unsafe to contact a deceased person directly, I ask my guides to act as go-betweens. I pose a question that they relay to the energy body of the deceased. After a few moments, they transmit any answers back to me. Safety is paramount. It's more secure to disappoint a client for being unable to contact a deceased person that day than to risk carrying that individual's spirit around inside your skin for decades. It's a frightening possibility but the answer is easy. Simply skip any mediumship practice and focus on other types of intuitive development.

Occasionally, when the energy body of a deceased person wants to communicate with me and I don't feel comfortable, I explain that if it has an important message for the world, it needs to be born into a physical body, mature into an adult and then tell people directly. Impatient types usually realise the endurance required to cope with time, temperature, gravity, hunger, emotions and family relationships. By the time many people reach adulthood, they have forgotten most of what they came to do in this life. What begins as a spiritual quest can easily settle into a desire to be comfortable.

Sometimes, after years of pursuing financial ease, opportunities or sudden disappointments awaken people to their deeper life purpose. The process has its own challenges, including the delicate balance between earning a living, keeping physically fit and pursuing a meaningful life. This process requires vigilance and occasional sacrifices, including releasing some friends who distract from an intended path in life. Sometimes it can be complicated to find meaningful work that aligns with our spiritual values.

Your life purpose doesn't have to be a vocation involving saving lives or helping people. Baking bread every morning for a café or working in a store are worthwhile careers if your life has purpose. Earning income only has to support you in a way that doesn't conflict with your personal spiritual values.

28.
YOUR UNIQUE INTUITIVE JOURNEY

The information this book provides can either be an interesting diversion from your daily demands or a personal turning point in your life path.

Perhaps the most significant concept this book offers is that of using personal intuition to notice opportunities. By aiming to identify even 10 per cent more possibilities per month, your life is likely to flourish in a year or two. Don't stop at 10 per cent. I challenge you to become aware of 60 per cent more openings — but fasten your seatbelt first.

If it's important to stay on your existing spiritual path, having effective strategies for sensitivity can reduce distractions. This means taking time to notice what foods make you fuzzy-headed, which people disturb your energy fields, how much daily exercise is required for a good night's sleep and how to remain nourished through positive sources of joy.

Listening to your physical body is a fundamental pillar for personal development because by doing this, you'll notice hidden agendas and also where your daily energy reserves are squandered. In paying attention to your physical being, you can quickly notice when it's tired, resentful or ready for change. This awareness reduces the possibility of being startled by life, because the body often senses change approaching before the mind is aware of it.

By asking better questions of your intuitive self, it's likely that you'll be more emotionally and mentally available for life. Essentially, you'll feel more alive each day. You'll also be taking more responsibility for your contribution to outcomes. Meaningful queries include:

- What do I most need to know right now?
- Is this path right for me spiritually?
- What am I not seeing in this situation?
- What is the right course of action in these circumstances?
- How can I forgive them for the pain I'm experiencing?
- What personal strengths can I develop now for a better future?

All of these enquiries avoid luck or fate and encourage personal effort to change life direction. Intuition isn't about finding lucky lotto numbers. It's better focused on noticing opportunities for personal growth and happiness. These chances exist but most people miss them while focusing on mundane activities.

When strengthening personal intuitive skills, practice is essential. Doing is learning, if you're paying attention. Naturally, you'll stumble at first while discovering your innate talents and honing reliable skills. This is where persistence is vital. Every day contains opportunities to practise intuitive development.

In the 1980s, I read at a local market most Saturdays for a few years. The market consisted of over 100 small stalls scattered around an old sandstone church in Sydney's eastern suburbs. Inside the church was a café providing fresh juices, loaves of crusty bread and the usual range of salads and hot food. I would set up my small, folding card table outside and cut the cards to ask if it would rain that day.

Sometimes I'd sit for an hour after setting up before reading for my first client. At first, I read books as I sat at the table but I noticed that passing potential clients didn't want to disturb me. Instead, I began to practise sliding the 78 cards across the table into an arc. Then, I learned to take one card at the end of a line and turn every card over. Instead of simply waiting for clients, it was an opportunity to expand skills that I'd use for the next 30 years.

Eventually, I developed a range of activities to make the most of any spare time on market days. I designed new business cards, outlined courses, drew up an appointment schedule for the day and more. It took over a year to realise that I could apply this system to every day of my life. Consequently, I produced seven books in a nine-year period. When feeling uninspired by teaching courses, I designed new ones that focused on skills I wanted to strengthen. Teaching others is a great way to better understand a subject. I had to discover games and exercises to help beginners grasp concepts and build confidence while developing new skills.

It took many years to train myself away from negative thinking. "What could go wrong with this opportunity?" is what I'd previously asked myself when positive openings presented themselves. This question is important when exploring new options but it can be limiting if it's the only question asked. To keep a balanced viewpoint, it's necessary to also ask:

- If this goes wrong, what are my options?
- How can I reduce the chance of this outcome occurring?
- If this conclusion is inevitable, is it still worthwhile pursuing?

Sometimes, pursuing a project that isn't successful helps to develop skills or business and creative contacts that support another venture to thrive. This isn't to diminish the disappointment felt when effort and planning don't bear fruit but rather to shorten the time between a collapsed plan and a new direction.

Keeping an intuitive diary makes some people think of a teenage girl, filling her days as she chronicles her life for a readership of one. Good record-keeping provides real data and often highlights our personal intuitive specialties. When events you've predicted a year ago begin to unfold in your daily life, it's handy to be able to retrieve your diary and read the actual predictions. It becomes obvious if you had the basic concept correct but not the fine details. Or, if you were correct about one aspect of events but didn't know what they signified because you didn't search for context at the time. This helps to refine your intuitive skills.

To strengthen your personal competence, find or establish a practice group. Over the decades, students in my courses who have gone on to become professional clairvoyants were usually those people who created a practice venue and invited fellow students to join them. The longest-running associations were created early in courses. In a three-Sunday intro course, if a student invited everyone to their house the following Saturday, perhaps one-third of the class turned up. However, after people talked about the Saturday experience at lunch on Sunday (during the course) more students wanted to attend the following week. I encouraged group organisers to request that every participant bring a friend so that fellow beginners would have strangers to read for. Reading for unknown people is a hurdle some students avoid but diving in with a team of beginners is the quickest way to improve.

In an advanced tarot course, Steph was excited to share her experience with a skills group. She invited her friend Frances for a three-hour Sunday practice session and they set off with an orange and poppyseed cake from a local patisserie. There were six other tarot readers when they arrived at Michael's house and they separated into different rooms to read in privacy. It's difficult to focus when you can hear another reader explaining a different card in the background. Readings averaged 20 minutes each. Everyone took a break two hours into the process and devoured the cake with tea and coffee. More clients arrived and departed throughout the day.

On the drive home, Steph asked Frances how it went for her. Frances explained that she had asked an important question about her relationship with Rick. She had six readings in the afternoon and asked six different people the same question. Their answers were the same — that Rick didn't want to make any more commitment than he was currently making and that another man might change her relationship landscape when he arrived in 18 months.

"Tarot actually works!" she declared passionately to the class.

"That's great. It means I haven't wasted the last 35 years reading the cards," I quipped.

GLOSSARY

Animal intuition

An instinctive intuition that is survival-oriented and common to animals. It often manifests as 'gut feelings', hunches or body sensations. It is not suitable for intricate predictions but can be used for 'Yes/No' questions in the moment.

Astral body

One of the finer energy forms. Although the astral body resembles the physical form, it is not subject to the same limitations of weight, temperature or the need for physical nourishment and sleep each day. It is an emotional body and forms part of a person's aura or fine energy field.

Astral travel

Excursions on the astral plane taken by the astral body. The astral body does not require sleep at night and can travel great distances during nocturnal slumbers. This can be to reunite with friends or to communicate with deceased loved ones.

Aura

The energy field that surrounds all living things, from individual leaves to animals and humans. These fine energy forms surround every person's body and contract when someone is ill or tired and expand when that individual is excited, angry or under the influence of alcohol.

Chakras

Taken from the ancient Sanskrit word for 'wheel' or 'disc', the word 'chakras' refers to the seven main energy vortices down the front amd back of the human body and a range of smaller, lesser-known energy wheels at the joints (knees, elbows, ankles etc.) Each of the main chakras represents different aspects of the human condition, including passion and enthusiasm, heartfelt love, mental curiosity, personal power, connection to spirit and connection to the earth.

Clairaudience

Meaning 'clear hearing', it is the ability to hear that still, small voice within. Clairaudience also enables psychics to listen to their spiritual guides or higher self in meditation or to internally pick up messages from the deceased friends of clients.

Clairvoyance

Meaning 'clear seeing', it is the ability to glimpse intuitive images in the mind's eye. These are distinguished in the same way that memories of past events are perceived — internally and not with the physical eyes.

Dross

Negativity, such as stress, anxiety, fear, anger, longstanding resentment or guilt. If you meditate in the same place regularly, it's best not to do this where others might sit or stand, as they may leave dross behind in your sacred space.

Higher self

The spiritual aspect of an individual that is aware of the karmic consequences of actions and is well placed to guide or advise that person with spiritual development and purpose.

Karma

The connection between cause and effect. Being aware of personal karma involves noticing how your choices or actions produce consequences, both for yourself and others. It also highlights how the negative repercussions of our actions can teach us about the value of living ethical lives.

Karmic cord

An invisible energy cord connecting two people due to the past unresolved actions of one or both of them. These cords often exist between parents and their children and between strangers who have spent time together in previous lives. Karmic cords cannot be broken until the karma is settled. Karma is concluded through understanding, atonement and forgiveness.

Kinaesthetic

Intuition that relies on the body sensations experienced when you enter a new location, sit next to a stranger or spend time in an unfamiliar room. Kinaesthetic intuitives are tactile psychics who naturally feel the health issues people around them are experiencing.

Master

See spiritual master.

Meditation

A state when the conscious mind is relaxed, the physical body is calm and it's possible to focus awareness inwardly, towards profound matters. Some people enter this state during slow, repetitive exercise, such as a long walk in a familiar setting.

Mediumship

The practice of being a psychic conduit between this world and the next. Psychic mediums can contact the deceased, often to reassure the living that the departed are fine in the afterlife.

Mentor

Someone experienced with intuitive skills and practices who can teach and guide people who are discovering their own spiritual purpose.

Psyche

This is an ancient word for 'soul' or 'spirit'. Traditionally, psychics looked into the hearts and souls of others, to gently advise them on how to release personal pain and to evolve spiritually.

Psychic cleansing

Also known as 'spiritual cleansing', this is a process of removing any dross or negative energy collected through daily living. Psychic cleansing helps the psyche or soul maintain a clear vision of your true self and your purpose in this life.

Psychic cord

Invisible, thin cords of energy that link us to others. Psychic energy cords are formed through desire — to be with someone, to be understood by another person or to influence others.

Psychic protection

The act of protecting yourself, your home or your workplace from surrounding negativity or any harmful intentions directed towards you by others.

Psychometry

The process of noticing and interpreting energies contained in an object by someone who has owned or repeatedly touched that object. Experienced psychometrists can intuit a psychic cord from the object to its owner and describe events in that person's life (see psychic cords).

Sleepers' class

A group of students whose bodies are asleep while their spiritual selves convene for lessons from experienced spiritual teachers. Often these pupils won't consciously remember night-time classes when they awaken.

Soul

A part of each living person that exists to deepen its understanding of the physical world while remembering that this journey is only temporary. When the soul departs the body, we die. It then returns to the spiritual world to reflect on the life recently ended and to evolve. Some people believe that each soul experiences hundreds or even thousands of lives to refine itself, whereas others believe that spirits require less than 20 lives to understand the human experience.

Spirit

See soul.

Spiritual guide

An invisible adviser, often between physical lives, who can provide independent guidance that is accessed through meditation or during dreams at night.

Spiritual intuition

Intuitive awareness that can highlight underlying causes of circumstances and reveal outcomes of current endeavours. Unlike animal intuition, which is restricted to the present moment, spiritual intuition allows you to move awareness back to past events and forward in time to future opportunities.

Spiritual master

Someone who has achieved spiritual mastery. This includes understanding the full consequences of their decisions and actions. It also involves physical, emotional, mental and spiritual self-nourishment. Spiritual masters are profoundly aware of their personal spiritual purpose.

Telepathy

From the word *tele* meaning 'distant' and *patheia* meaning 'to be affected by'. This is the process of sending or receiving images or information at a distance without any communication devices. It's also described as sending mental messages. Telepathy is most effective when the sender and receiver are good friends or of the same mind.

Visual

Visual intuition or clairvoyance (meaning 'clear seeing') is the ability to see intuitive images in the mind's eye. These might be scenes in foreign countries, in the future, or of deceased people.

ABOUT THE AUTHOR

When asked how he became a clairvoyant, Paul Fenton-Smith admits he didn't see it coming. He began his intuitive exploration in 1978 at age 17 when a friend enrolled him in a palmistry course. His initial scepticism faded in lesson three when the teacher described his nature clearly, based on the shape and flexibility of his thumbs.

In the decades since, Paul has studied tarot card reading, astrology, psychic development, clinical hypnotherapy and counselling, combining these into his private practice. Paul founded the Academy of Psychic Sciences in 1985. The course notes provided to students have been the basis for 13 published books that take a practical approach to these esoteric subjects. Paul's books include vivid examples from life to inspire readers to try each method themselves.

Aside from his teaching commitments at the Academy, Paul runs a busy private practice in Sydney as a clairvoyant, counsellor and hypnotherapist and conducts courses internationally. Through practising and teaching intuitive studies for more than 40 years, Paul encourages his clients and students to believe only what they can see or experience for themselves.

www.paulfentonsmith.com

ADVANCED TAROT

An In-depth Guide to Practical & Intuitive Tarot Reading

PAUL FENTON-SMITH

This in-depth study of the tarot explores the symbolism, meanings and interpretation of all 78 cards of the tarot alongside anecdotes and insights drawn from decades of reading and teaching experience.

Enhance your knowledge of traditional meanings with intuitive impressions for clear, supportive and insightful readings. Understand the reading process, word questions for more accurate readings and answer Yes/No questions with confidence.

- Upright and reversed meanings for general, career, relationship and health questions for every single card
- Essential questions menu
- Range of go-to layouts
- Sample interpretations
- Quick reference charts and correspondences
- Full-colour images from the Rider-Waite Tarot

A one-stop resource for tarot newbies and those wanting to take their readings to a professional level. Renowned author and teacher, Paul Fenton-Smith has over 40 years' experience and is the founder of the Academy of Psychic Sciences in Sydney. Whether reading for clients, teaching or conveying his knowledge through his books, Paul's insightful and practical approach brings clear benefits to people's everyday lives.

556 pages, paperback book
ISBN: 978-0-648746-82-9

ALSO AVAILABLE FROM BLUE ANGEL PUBLISHING®

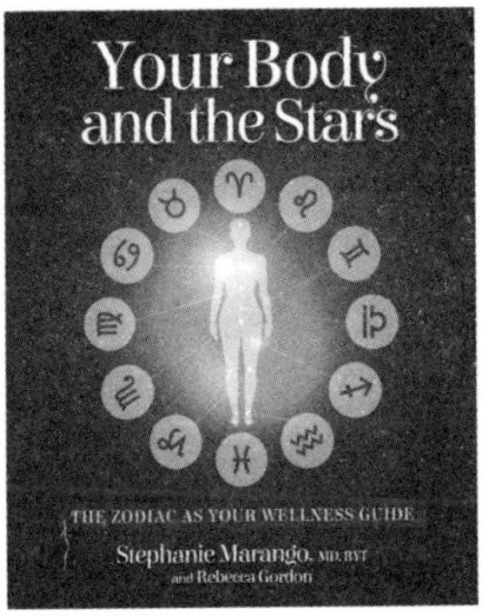

YOUR BODY AND THE STARS

The Zodiac as your Wellness Guide

STEPHANIE MARANGO & REBECCA GORDON

Your Body and the Stars is a fun and insightful handbook that takes a revolutionary approach to wellness by unlocking the power of the stars. Working through the twelve zodiac signs and the body region each sign represents—from head (Aries) to toe (Pisces)—discover how to give your body the attention it deserves.

Do you suffer from neck pain? Go to the chapter on Taurus to learn why your neck hurts. Want healthier knees? Learn preventive exercises in the Capricorn chapter. This is the first comprehensive, self-directed holistic program that covers emotional and mental health along with the body. Identify your sun sign or a body region that needs care, and then draw on the zodiac's wisdom for practical tips and illustrated exercises (based on a mix of yoga, stretch and strengthening movements, and Pilates) that deliver an effective result.

Your Body and the Stars brings together medically trained, holistic physician Dr. Stephanie Marango and talented astrologist Rebecca Gordon, whose astrology columns appear on numerous websites and publications. Marango and Gordon combine their individual expertise to bridge the zodiac signs to physical life, providing a lifelong tool that can both prevent illness and optimize wellbeing, illuminating your head-to-toe healing connection to the cosmos.

226 pages, paperback book
ISBN: 978-1-925538-05-2

PRACTICAL MAGIC

An Oracle for Everyday Enchantment

SERENE CONNEELEY

Artwork by Selina Fenech

Energise the purpose, knowledge, and potential within you to empower your heart and transform your tomorrows. This inspired collaboration is a rich compendium of fascination, insight, ritual, symbolism, and divination that you can action in your daily life for surprising and satisfying results.

- Beautiful artworks specially created to reflect the meaning and alchemy of each card.
- Step-by-step spellwork, visualisations, associations, and exercises for ushering in a charmed life.
- A comprehensive magical resource for creating sacred space, understanding moon phases, working with Nature's cycles, influencing your future, and more.

Journey into initiation and possibility, welcome adventure and reward, set nurturing boundaries, and shape your reality with the support of deities, herbs, crystals, colour, the elements, and intention. Believe in your innate powers of creation and innovation, and charge your world with wonder — now and always.

Set includes 36 full-colour cards, 304-page guidebook & card stand packaged in a hardcover box with magnetic close.

36 cards, 304-page guidebook + card stand set
ISBN: 978-1-922573-70-4

UNVEILING THE GOLDEN AGE
A Visionary Tarot Experience

IZZY IVY

An alchemic gateway of tarot, vision, empowerment and expansive play.

Traverse portals, glide down rainbows and feel the glory of your wings in this truly revelationary tarot and meditation deck. Intricate and intuitive, startling and reassuring, this 78-card offering was birthed from physical and multi-dimensional realms to ground and elevate the reader in a synergy of co-creative connection.

Izzy Ivy's unique divinatory system offers insight, direction, healing practices and recalibration for yourself and others. There are also supports for leading group meditations and accessing collective wisdom and visions. However you connect with the hand-painted wonders and spirit-led guidance, your journey with the Golden Age will be natural, timely and deeply transformative.

78 cards with gold-painted edges + full-colour 304-page guidebook set
ISBN: 978-1-922573-74-2